Praise for *Sp*

If you are a professional speaker or su ...., ... your first speech, this book is the most valuable resource available for your speaker journey. No matter what your vocation is, speaking is the best way to attract clients, generate leads and grow your business. Your message is your gift to the world, and through the structured training in this book you will learn skills to prepare you for any impromptu or professional speaking situation. Arvee includes real life examples of the components of your speech as well as tips to create a persuasive presentation that will have clients pursuing you. The cherry on the sundae is the Appendices Section which contains templates for your One Sheet as well as for bookings, introductions, marketing, closings and referrals. "Speak Up, Get Clients" is the complete package that will equip you for your life as a persuasive, sought-after speaker.

Diane Watson

Speak Up, Get Clients *is absolutely superb both in its sharing of ideas and in the way they are presented in the book. Arvee Robinson convincingly shares her gift as a Master Speaker Trainer guiding the reader with clear and distinct step-by-step examples of how we can all use the art of Public Speaking as a marketing strategy to grow our business; and to improve and retain our customer base. Ultimately, she empowers readers to discover how they can tap into the true power of Public Speaking.*

Carol Metz Murray, Chief Engagement Officer

Arvee Robinson's contributions as a public speaker, speaker trainer, and now author, enable us to accomplish a transformation and give us the courage, confidence and flexibility to be both self-reliant and interdependent through the gift of our own voices. This beautifully written book, in my opinion, clarifies and captures Arvee's intention and vision to enable her readers to embrace vulnerability, so that we become leaders who possess common sense, conviction, compassion, sympathy and can create a duplicable blueprint for profound self-introductions and signature presentations. I am happy her influence as a mentor and trainer has now transcended as an author. Anyone who wishes to spawn ideas toward activities that enable people collectively to bring forth innate potential with fresh and dynamic vitality must read this book!

Your Padowan, Jason Christopher
Financial Educator and College Consultant

An outstanding read about how a person can achieve success in becoming a great public speaker with presentations often made within the zone of excellence. The author addresses the negative factors which diminish performances and instill fear of public speaking into many talented persons. Candidates start with learning the basic principles and building a framework to abound in self-confidence to be a competent speaker in a variety of circumstances. A careful set of formulas takes the mystery out of delivering great public speeches that are appropriate, persuasive, and effective to market, sell, and present products, services, and new ideas. The shared client scenarios demonstrate how successful the methodologies are in different real situations. The author's sharing of both personal growth and professional experience makes the reading rich and most interesting. I recommend highly this book if you want to overcome doubt and prove how great of a public speaker you can become.

Frederick W. James MD
Founder: PowerSpending Academy

This is more than a self-help book. Arvee goes above and beyond regular book writing. She transcends Readers from Mediocre to professional view of speaking without being boring. The reader is taken on a discovery journey and a self-searching experience that turns public speaking into a money-making machine. Arvee has riveting and humorous style that quickly catches one's attention. I highly recommend this easy to read book to all business owners.

Janet Kazibwe

Speak Up, Get Clients *stands above as Arvee Robinson's gift to the world, and to your life. This powerful book reveals How-To steps that enable ordinary people to have an extraordinary impact on others' lives. The author, a gifted transformational coach, gently, lovingly removes our excuses for not speaking our truth. God bless you, Arvee Robinson!"*

Rich Kozak, RichBrands
Brand Architect and Strategist

Arvee Robinson's Speaker Training Intensive is the best training I have ever had and I was trained by the best. Nothing I've ever received from one of the most successful sales training programs in corporate America came close to matching Arvee's knowledge, passion, enthusiasm and humor. I would recommend this book as a must read to anyone who agrees that speaking engagements are the best way to get leads and there are a lot of people who see this that would have never thought about it before. I certainly didn't. Her training is transformative, and one can't help but leave with the knowledge that their life has been changed in a most meaningful way.

Tina Dipane

I adore Arvee and, while I've worked through Toastmasters, Arvee brings another level to speaking and especially developing a business from the stage. With her book, we finally have the notes to support her talks along with actionable ideas to build our speaking skills and income. This book is so full of content that it may take a few read thoughts to take it all in. A solid and must read for anyone who has to sell themselves or their ideas from the stage."

Elizabeth Gilbert, Photographer

Bar none, the the fastest way to influence others persuasively is to learn how to speak from the stage--AND Arvee Robinson excels at this like none other. After all, she is known by insiders in the speaking industry as the trainer who trains those who do speaker training themselves. And even better, she has an accelerated system to get anyone ready to step on stage for the first time, a plan to do it confidently and successfully. A business owner for the past 15 years, I whole-heartedly agree with Arvee that the fastest way to attract high paying clients is to learn how to package and present your own presentation before a live audience. You will want to use this book as your training guide to fast track your message into your market place with your own unique competitive advantage. You will also love the scripts for booking speaking engagements to Chambers of Commerce, as well as business and not-for-profit organizations. Arvee also includes her speaker introduction template, speaker one-sheet, and all the other assets that every speaker needs to thrive as a powerful, influential presenter in your market place. This book is the key to unlocking your message, and fast tracking your career as a speaker. Furthermore, what I love about the training Arvee provides in this book, is how comprehensive her system is for pulling a message out, and framing it in a way that allows anyone to confidently create a presentation that rocks! And what you won't realize until you purchase the book, is that Arvee provides private video training to help you put her entire system together. Get this book and use it today as your road map to success for your next presentation!

Glenn Dietzel

Arvee Robinson has written a must-read for business owners who want to use speaking to get more clients. Her easy-to-use system for writing compelling speeches turns a potentially daunting task into a simple process that anyone can follow. If you want to begin speaking or are a seasoned speaker you will find this book filled with nuggets you cannot get anywhere else.

Bethany Sunny
Thriving Business Success

Thank you so much Arvee for not only teaching me the importance of finding my voice, but also showing me how to use it so that I can impact the lives of people who God has prepared to hear the message He has for me to share with them. Arvee, you are an awesome trainer and an even more awesome woman of faith!

Bill Cross
Background Screening Solutions

If you are a speaker or aspire to be one, you have found the right book! As a Loving Relationship Coach and Speaker, I have to say that **Speak Up, Get Clients** is long overdue! Arvee Robinson has been my speaker trainer and mentor since 2009, and I have received so much value from her training. However, this book brings everything to LIFE. It is a generous compilation of every tip, tool, and system this energetic, powerhouse trainer teaches in her classes, workshops, and masterminds!

This book is a MUST read for anyone who wants to up their game in the speaking arena!

Sandy Ireland
Loving Relationship Coach and Speaker

Arvee's "Speech Sandwich" is pure genius! I have gone from a Good Speaker to a Great Speaker by following her System on "How to Craft a Speech."

D'Lee Mayberry C.A.S.
Professional Speaker

Here's a fact you can't argue with: If you're service professional looking to grow your business, Public Speaking is absolutely, hands down, the best way to quickly gain a lot of visibility, develop a credible expert brand, and attract new clients. And **Speak Up, Get Clients** *is a $2,000 course - teaching you everything you need to know to get booked, wow your audience, and go home with new clients and sales - packed into a $20 book! Get it right NOW! Arvee Robinson, a two-decades-in-the-trenches Master Speaker Trainer, must have lost her mind to put so much of her insider knowledge in a $20 book! From selecting the right topics and getting invited to speak in front of your ideal clients, to crafting presentations that will wow the crowd, to tips on turning even a few minutes on stage into an avalanche of new sales - this book tells all. Plus, Arvee will have you spellbound by her riveting stories and excited to take action and follow the countless "copy and deploy" tips, templates and case studies! If you are an entrepreneur -buy this book now.*

Adam Urbanski
The Marketing Mentor

I loved Arvee from the moment she opened her mouth. Literally!!! As a holistic health coach specializing in weight loss, asthma and diabetes, when I saw her on stage and knew I wanted to work with her, so I could expand my programs and help more people. I hired her to help me SPEAK UP and love her course and couldn't wait to read **Speak Up, Get Clients**. *Arvee LOADED this book with her top-secret tools to help you attract new clients every time you speak. A must read for every level speaker.*

Becca Tebon
speaker, coach and author

Arvee takes the art of speechification to a new level with her practical, step-by-step approach. Let her take your hand and gently walk you through everything you need to know to get your speech written, practiced and polished. Arvee's proven system is simple, usable, and foolproof, and one you are sure to turn to over and over again!

Donna Loeffler
Professional speaker and coach

Speak Up,
Get Clients

How to Use
Public Speaking as a
Marketing Strategy to
Attract High-paying Clients

Arvee Robinson

The Master Speaker Trainer

Speak Up, Get Clients
Published by Solutions Press
Newport Beach, California

ISBN: 978-0-9996947-1-8

First edition printed December 2017

Printed in the United States of America

This is a work of non-fiction. The ideas presented are those of the author alone. All references to possible results discussed in this book relate to specific past examples and are not representative of any future results specific individuals may achieve.

Introduction

Most people are either so afraid to speak in public that they never get started or they are so confident they step on stage with no idea what they are doing.

Either way, they fail.

Speaking is not a sport for amateurs. It's a profession.

And like all professions you need comprehensive training to succeed. But not any kind of training. You need structured training that includes a step-by-step system that you can replicate for every speech you give.

Persuasive speaking is complicated. To succeed on stage, you need more than a beginning, middle, and end. You need to know how to eliminate the fear of speaking, how to become a great storyteller, and how to exude confidence.

You also need to know why you are speaking, your desired outcome, and the next steps you want your audience to take.

I designed this book to train you in skills you can use to attract new clients, generate unlimited leads, and grow your business every time you speak.

Everything you need is in this book. You will learn my step-by-step system to craft your speech, how to get speaking engagements, and six different closes that attract clients.

You will also get templates, forms, and scripts that will make it easy to get speaking engagements, prepare any type of speech, and close any audience.

Your training starts here, in Chapter 1.

Acknowledgements

A heartfelt thank you to my best friend, business partner, and book coach, Lee Pound, for his patience, expertise, time, and love as we worked side-by-side, collaborating word by word, page by page, chapter by chapter to make this the best public speaking book possible. Without his help this book would not have been written.

I'm forever grateful to the love of my life, my husband Michael Jakubowski, for believing in me and giving his never-ending encouragement, patience, and love.

Foreword

By Lee Pound
The Write Coach, CSL Writers Workshop

Public speaking is the single best way to establish yourself as an expert in your field and attract clients to your business.

Arvee Robinson's speaker system, revealed in this book, gives novice speakers, even those afraid to step on stage, tools to build confidence, create a speech that sells, and position themselves as the best in their market.

Speaking from the stage is a profession. You need training in the skills that will make you shine from the stage. Having worked with Arvee for over 15 years and having used her system myself, I know she is the best in the business at training speakers.

She honed her speaking skills in the corporate world, then opened her speaker training business 15 years ago. For six years she and I presented the Speak Your Way to Wealth seminars, designed to introduce new speakers to the world of speaking from the stage. She now offers a four-day speaker training program, private speaker coaching, and advanced business mastermind programs.

Before you say your first words from the stage, read this book, learn Arvee's system, practice the skills she presents, and build a signature presentation that will wow your audience.

You will be amazed how quickly Arvee's techniques make you a confident, effective speaker who attracts clients every time you speak.

Dedication

To all my students
who listened carefully,
practiced diligently,
spoke confidently
and made a ton of money.

Table of Contents

Part I

The Message:
Why You Must Speak Up

1

Guided to the Right Path

Public speaking is the best way to get clients. Whose life are you going to change today with your words?
--Arvee Robinson

Public speaking is the best way to get clients and customers for your business and share your beliefs and passions with the world.

For many years, in every job I had, I spoke to get customers but locked away the part of me that longed to express my personal beliefs and passions. I gave good speeches, full of valuable information but without passion.

This book tells how I married these two aspects of speaking and how you can too.

I first stepped onto the stage as an aspiring actress, a role I played for over four years. To be clear, acting and speaking are different. In acting you play another person using words you didn't write. In speaking, you play yourself and use your words and ideas to persuade others to work with you, buy your products, or buy into your ideas and passions.

One day, driving to yet another audition, I noticed for the first time One Wilshire, a 30-story building with dark windows on white lattice at Wilshire and Grand in downtown Los Angeles.

"I want to work there," I thought to myself as I passed it.

After my audition (no role again), I contacted a recruiter to start a serious job search. I was tired of the constant rejection for situations I had no control over like being too short or too old for the role. I was tired of push-starting my VW bug because I didn't have the money to buy a new starter. I was tired of being broke. I needed to get a real job. A couple of days later my recruiter called and I was shocked when I discovered she had found a secretarial job in that same building I drove past two days earlier, the One Wilshire building!

Excited, I started the best paying role ever, as a secretary to three mangers for a large international CPA firm, Deloitte Haskins and Sells. I'd never been a secretary, so I approached the challenge as if playing a role. I asked myself, "What do I need to do to be the best secretary they have ever seen?"

My edge was my inadvertent computer background where I assisted the head programmer as he programmed the company's custom system to run on a mainframe computer (this was back in the day when computer systems took up an entire room). How did a secretary in the Small Business Department get this job? They had a large investment in a new-fangled Apple computer, which they kept in an office under lock and key. They wanted me to find out how they could use it. Soon I took charge of the key to that locked room and, as it turned out, to the wave of the future, computing.

I loved my new career and was good at it. Within six months one of my bosses, Don Nelson, said to me, "I noticed you're inputting client's accounting information into their computers."

Let me clarify, the early 1980s were a revolutionary time when microcomputers first arrived on the scene. The thought of becoming a data operator, going to clients every day, and typing all day didn't appeal to me.

I looked at my boss and replied, "Why don't we teach them how to do it?!"

He embraced the idea, had it approved by the managing partner, and created my dream job! I was a microcomputer systems consultant (another great paying role).

I was a trailblazer because no one in the industry provided this service. There were no classes I could take so I took the DOS (Disk Operating System) manual and taught myself the commands.

At the time, I learned the two accounting systems that worked on IBM microcomputers inside and out. I remember I set up my first accounting system on a dual floppy computer. Hard disks did not yet exist.

One day a few months later, as I taught myself new accounting software, my boss Don called me into his office again and said, "Arvee, we want you to speak to business organizations to bring in more clients to build our systems consulting practice."

I thought to myself, "Piece of cake!" I took one speech class in college, so I knew how to speak in public. I was good to go. Or so I thought.

After six months of speaking, I hadn't landed one new client. For the life of me, I didn't know what was wrong.

One day, I stood in the back of the room after my speech and watched all my potential clients walk out the door. I thought, "No sales again. Don's going to demote me right back to my secretarial job if I don't get moving."

That's when a woman tapped me on the shoulder and said, "Honey, I hate to tell you this…"

Then don't! I thought to myself, because I knew nothing good would come out of her mouth.

I asked, "Tell me what?"

"Did you know that after every sentence you say 'okay'?!"

I stared at her, speechless. All I could say was, "Okay."

At that moment, I got it. I was my own distraction. My audience never heard my message. They were too busy counting okays!

I could have quit right then, but didn't.

Instead, I decided to master public speaking. I read every book I could find, took classes, went to seminars, and hired a coach.

As I implemented the lessons I learned, I was amazed. I attracted new clients every time I spoke.

Public speaking works.

Overnight my systems consulting practice expanded and I had to hire staff to handle all the new business. My colleagues noticed my success and asked, "What are you doing?"

I set up a series of lunch and learn sessions where I taught them what I had learned. They made more sales too.

Soon after, I got a call from the managing partner, the big boss, the one you never see unless you are in trouble. He invited me up to his corner office on the 29th floor. Oops, I thought. I realized I never got permission to host the lunch and learns, use their supplies and equipment, or teach outside approved corporate training classes.

I walked into his office and closed the door behind me.

"Please sit down," he said. He motioned toward a chair in front of his mahogany desk.

I sat with my hands clasped.

"I hear what you are doing." He paused. "And I like it!"

I breathed.

"I want you to teach these skills to our American managers and supervisors," he said, "so they can go out and get more clients too."

Twice a year the firm flew me to Chicago and Arizona to develop and teach continuing education workshops to these supervisors and managers. I loved every minute.

At another firm, I created a new series of intensive workshops to teach my colleagues how to use public speaking to attract more clients.

Public speaking became my passion.

I used public speaking throughout my 23-year career in corporate America to attract clients, close sales, and build my consulting group. I used it in management meetings, staff interviews and evaluations, and to climb to the top of the corporate ladder.

During the last few years, I realized I was no longer making a difference in my industry or blazing trails. I could do little that my staff couldn't do better and cheaper. I had become a corporate robot trapped in an industry saturated with systems consultants and under ever-increasing pressure to produce more and more.

I wanted out. However, I didn't want to exchange one corporate cocoon for another. I also wanted to keep the big corporate salary, the BMW, and the prestige. The prospect of walking away from all of it was scary.

I decided to start my own company. I explored personal fitness, fengshui, and private consulting, and planned to use public speaking to build it. Which to choose? I did what any smart woman would do, I prayed about it. The answer surprised me – forget all the others and teach public speaking to business owners.

"Ah-ha! That's it." I thought to myself.

For months, in my spare time, I worked on creating the business of my dreams. I hired a graphic artist who created a logo, business card, and letterhead designs. I worked with a business coach to set up the infrastructure for my business. I was ready to start.

Then I chickened out!

Friday, October 31, 2003, I was going to march into my boss's office and resign. My plan was to share with him how I received a higher calling. I never got the chance.

I was out in the field that day and although I had plenty of time to get back into the office, I didn't. The truth was, I didn't have the guts to tell my boss, who I adored, that I planned to leave. I rationalized that because the firm was moving to a new location it would be better for me to move with them and resign in a month or two. I prayed for strength.

God answered my prayer.

Monday morning my boss called me into his office. We're going to talk about client projects, I thought.

"Please sit down." he said.

Then he hit me with it. "We are eliminating your department."

I was shocked! The only word I could think to say was, "Okay." But I resisted.

I stood and walked out of his office. I thought, "He took away my power!" Then a quiet voice spoke to me, "No. He gave you your power!"

I didn't have the guts to quit so God gave me a gentle shove out the door and guided me to the right path.

2

How Speaking Can Change Your Life and Your Business

Your message is your gift to the world. It costs you nothing and buys you everything.
--Arvee Robinson

Like many entrepreneurs who come out of corporate careers, I was passionate about helping people, but I knew little about starting a business.

The moment I walked out of my job, I had a sense of total freedom! After punching a time clock for so many years, it felt like I had all the time in the world. I hung out my shingle and volunteered to be Division Governor for my district in Toastmasters, started a storytelling club, joined a network marketing company, you name it, I did it, except work with clients. With this newfound freedom, I thought, I could do whatever I wanted, whenever I wanted. After several months of living off my savings, I realized I was doing it all wrong.

Months earlier while still working my day job, I attended Adam Urbanski's two-day seminar, *Small Biz Marketing Summit*. Adam talked about marketing. He spoke about building your database, your brand, and your marketing funnel. I had no clue what he was talking about. When I left the room that day, I thought, "I'll figure this out. How hard could it be?" After all, I've prospected, marketed, and closed clients for the past 23 years in corporate America.

I never did figure it out on my own.

One day, I glanced at my bookshelf and the notebook from Adam's seminar jumped out at me. I opened it, read through it and realized I couldn't implement it on my own. I called Adam and hired him as my mentor to help me make sense of this entrepreneurial marketing process.

During our first coaching call, I said, "Here's my problem, I started my business several months ago and I haven't attracted any coaching clients. What am I doing wrong?"

"How are you spending your time?" Adam asked.

With much excitement, I shared with him all the activities I was involved in.

"No wonder you don't have any business!" he said. "You're too busy being busy! If it doesn't produce clients, don't do it."

He paused for a second, then asked, "What do you teach your clients?"

"How to get clients with public speaking," I answered.

"Then why aren't you practicing what you preach?"

That question changed my life. I had never thought to use what I taught.

The minute I hung up, I called the program chairs of every organization I knew and set up a speaking schedule.

If I had not hired Adam as my mentor, I would have run back to corporate America with my tail between my legs. Thank God that didn't happen.

My first speech, to a group of high-powered bankers, attorneys, and consultants, was 30 minutes on how to deliver a persuasive speech. I don't remember the exact title, but I do remember I landed two clients that day. Afterwards, I reminded myself, "Public speaking worked in corporate America and it works for entrepreneurs, too."

I built a 6-figure income using public speaking to market my services. To this day, I speak one or two times a week to bring in new clients.

You too can use public speaking as a marketing strategy to attract clients, generate leads, and grow your business. All you need is knowledge and passion. You can learn the rest.

Jill was petrified to speak in public but knew she had to do it to attract clients. She came to me for help. Our first task was to define her target market. Her research revealed that her best clients would be women who are already healthy and wanted to be healthier. I asked her where those women would hang out. She zeroed in on Whole Foods Market, which caters to people interested in better nutrition, and called the store manager to schedule her presentation.

Together, Jill and I crafted her speech. She practiced it until she had the confidence to deliver it without fear.

When the big day came, she established herself as an instant authority on women's health with a 30-minute speech to 15 ladies that taught them how to eat right and stay healthy.

As time was running out she remembered me saying, "The more time you spend in front of the audience the more they fall in love with you and the more sales you make." She thought to herself, "I need more time with these women."

Then she had a brilliant idea! "Wouldn't it be great if I showed them around the store?" She invited them to join her for a tour of the market. "I'll show you what brands of healthy food to buy and where to find it."

Seven women took her up on the offer.

The next day she called these seven women and turned five of them into paying clients. Since she recommends supplements and food that they purchase from her, the life-time value of one client can be thousands of dollars. Jill can use the skills I taught her to create these same results for the rest of her life.

Why speaking works:

1. Speaking positions you as an expert in your field.

What is the main draw at professional or business meetings? Not the networking or rubber chicken. It's the guest speaker. He or she is the highlight of the meeting, the person who promises to give the attendees new insights into topics they want to understand at a deeper level.

To attract a large audience to the meeting, the organization sends several notices to their full list, members or not, to promote the speaker's unique expertise with a biography, a picture, and the title and description of the talk. This gives the speaker instant credibility.

When the audience walks through the door, they know the speaker is an expert.

2. Speaking allows your audience to fall in love with you.

When you speak, your audience gets to know you as a person through your personal story, words, actions, and body language. They resonate with your energy. The longer you speak the better they get to know you and the quicker they will fall in love with you and become life-long clients and customers.

3. Speaking is an inexpensive marketing strategy.

Marketing strategies are expensive. People pay thousands of dollars for fancy websites, expensive postcards and flyers, and advertising.

My first year in business, I didn't spend the money on a website or professional marketing materials. I built my business by speaking, which costs a little time and the gasoline to get there.

I often got that money back by getting a free meal or selling a book or product. And every time I walked away with new clients.

4. Speaking is an effortless way to build your database.

A database is one of the most powerful marketing tools you will ever create. It consists of names, email addresses, and phone numbers of people who will welcome your promotion of products and services because they saw you speak.

I use a strategy that has allowed me to build my database from zero to over 10,000 names in less than 10 years. Now I market to them by email or telemarketing. Since they have heard me speak either live, on a webinar, or on a teleseminar, they know me, tend to stay on my list for years and eventually buy.

5. Speaking is leverage.

The best way to leverage your time is to get in front of more people.

Most entrepreneurs schedule one-on-one appointments with every prospect they meet but close few. If you spent on average of half an hour with each prospect, it would take you 15 hours to talk to 30 people. When you speak to groups, you talk to all 30 people in one half-hour speech. This is a group screening process. At the end of your speech the cool prospects will leave and on average five hot prospects will approach you for more information. This leverages your time because you schedule appointments with the hot prospects. Speaking pre-qualifies every appointment you make, which increases the likelihood of a sale.

Imagine yourself speaking four times a month to groups of 30 people in your target market. In one month, you talk to 120 prospects. Of those 120, you can expect 20 hot leads. Let's be conservative and say out of the 20 you close 12. If one transaction is worth $2,500, the result is $30,000 in extra revenue per month. If you speak four times per month for twelve months you will reach 1,440 more people and bring in an extra $360,000 in new business!

That is counting one transaction per new client. Most new clients purchase more than one product or service. If our 1,440 new clients buy on average five items during their lifetime as a customer, each one will spend $12,500, or $18 million for all of them.

That's a lot of money.

Public speaking works for every business if you learn what to say, how to say it and where to say it.

3

How to Use Free Local Talks to Create a Flood of New Clients and Customers

Speaking to audiences eager to hear your message will attract high-paying clients and customers.
--Arvee Robinson

The audience sat on the edge of their seats, laughing. Not what you expect from an accountant.

One month earlier, my accountant Pete Elena was in my office working on my books. When I returned to the office after lunch, he said, "Hey that one-day speaker training you had last month was amazing! You got me thinking, in fact you got me out speaking to small groups like you said to do."

"So how is it going?" I asked.

"I'm giving speeches but I'm not getting any leads and I don't know what's wrong."

After an hour of private coaching to correct his mistakes, he said, "Okay, I got it!"

Now Pete's on stage at the Upland Chamber of Commerce and I'm laughing at his surprising natural humor. He was confident and having fun in front of his peers, clients, and people he'd known for years.

I was amazed as he wove dry humor into a boring subject, income tax, without slides, handouts, or notes. His audience roared with laughter the entire time.

After his talk, half a dozen people surrounded him, so I didn't interrupt him. The next day he called me. "Wow! I got four new tax return clients on the spot and three more prospects called me this morning. Thank you, thank you, thank you."

Pete charges $250 per tax return, an easy $1,000 in less than thirty minutes. He added, "Once a client hires me they stay with me. When you add services like bookkeeping, payroll, and bank reconciliation, the client's lifetime value could be over $25,000."

This is how the free local talk strategy works. You show up, speak for free, and generate leads that you convert into high-paying clients.

Who do I speak to?

The fastest way to get clients using this strategy is to speak in front of your target market. If you're not sure who your target market is, you need to pick one that you can relate to and that can relate to you.

Brenda is in the competitive field of financial planning. In our discussion of her potential niche in this huge market, we talked about who she serves best. She said everyone. I told her, "Everyone means no one. Who do you relate to the most?

She said, "Grandmothers, because I'm a grandmother."

Ah-ha, that was it. She can play in this target market. She understands grandmothers and they understand her. Her passion became clear: help grandparents create an investment fund for their grandchildren's future.

Play in the field where you have a clear advantage over your competition and where you can stand out.

When you know your target market, ask yourself where they hang out. For instance, Jill found her target market, healthy women who want to stay healthy, at a specialized location, Whole Foods Market.

You will find your target market in either a formal organization or specialized group you create.

Formal organizations

Find out which networking organization includes your target market, contact them, and ask to speak. For instance, I speak at high-end Chambers of Commerce because business owners are my target market.

Adrienne Dorig, a kitchen and bathroom designer, scheduled a speech at a Claremont Chamber of Commerce breakfast meeting to promote her business to a wide variety of affluent professionals, her natural clientele. Most of the members of that chamber fit into her niche so she was excited with the possibilities.

Before her talk, she called me. "I'm speaking next month," she said, "and I don't know how to make kitchen and bathroom design interesting. Help!"

My first thought was, "She's right. I'm not sure I'd sit through a program like that either."

However, I knew what she needed. She had five minutes to speak so we needed to make every second count. Using my system, we crafted a powerful attention grabber, a three-minute personal story that showed how her award-winning designs helped her clients create living spaces they never wanted to leave, and an invitation to the audience.

Two weeks later she delivered her five-minute talk and closed a $5,000 kitchen design project. That's $1,000 per minute.

When you use my speaking methods, it doesn't matter how much time they give you to speak. You attract more clients faster. Later in this book, I will teach you my speaker system, which allows you to prepare an effective speech of any length.

The thousands of organizations, associations, and corporations that host weekly or monthly meetings all over the country have created a huge demand for experts to speak on a wide variety of topics.

You can also reach a more specialized audience by creating your own group.

When I first met Donavan Price, an escrow officer, he said, "I'm struggling to get and keep new clients."

"Have you tried public speaking?" I asked.

He said no and asked how my speaker programs worked.

After a quick strategy session, he signed up for my speaker training intensive. He was a diligent student who did what I asked of him. At the end of four days, he walked out the door with a persuasive speech ready to deliver.

Two weeks later, an excited Donavan called me. "I got eight new clients!" he said.

Donavan's target market is real estate professionals, loan officers and financial advisors. He'd been meeting with them one at a time, a slow way to get business. "If I could get in front of more realtors at the same time," Donavan thought, "I'd get clients a lot faster."

He already participated in an established realtor industry event, a weekly caravan meeting. "Why not create one of my own," he thought, "and invite my prospects?" At his first meeting, 150 professionals showed up. Every Wednesday morning from then on Donavan spoke in front of his target niche, increased his visibility, and attracted new clients.

Two months later he called again and with even greater excitement said, "I bought a boat!" He emailed me a picture that looked more like a yacht than a boat.

Donavan was 21 years old when he learned my speaker system. He can use it to attract clients and make money for the rest of his life, no matter what business he is in.

Examples of both types of groups:

- Service clubs (Rotary, Lions, and Kiwanis)
- Meet-up groups
- Professional associations
- Networking groups
- Companies and Corporations
- Chambers of Commerce
- Industry groups
- Trade shows
- Conferences and seminars
- Vendor expos
- Health fairs
- Caravans
- Writers groups
- Churches
- Schools and Universities
- Home parties
- Informational meetings

Examples of professional organizations are American Institute of Certified Public Accountants (AICPA), National Association of Estate Planners & Councils (NAEPC), The National Association of Personal Financial Advisors (NAPFA), among others.

If your target market is women, you will find an abundance of women's associations and networking groups to choose from. A few examples are:

- National Association of Women Business Owners (NAWBO)
- American Business Women's Association (ABWA)
- International Association of Administrative Professionals (IAAP)
- National Association of Women Professionals (NAWP)
- Christian Women in the Media Association (CWIMA)
- Executive Women International (EWI)
- Women's Council of Realtors (WCR)

Wherever you choose to speak, make sure it includes your target market. The more targeted your audience, the more clients you'll attract.

4

Eliminate Stage Fright Forever!

FEAR is Fatal Expectations Altering Reality.
--Arvee Robinson

My worst nightmare came true 10 minutes into my first speech. My mind went blank. I fumbled with my notes. 300 people stared back at me. Seconds felt like minutes.

Months earlier, when a national software convention invited me to be a guest speaker, I was excited. My first break into the corporate speaking circuit.

The day came. Five of my peers and competitors shared the stage with me. Each of us spoke about the strengths of the accounting software system we represented. I spoke next to last.

I walked out on stage with confidence and put my notes on the lectern. For the first ten minutes, all went well. And then it happened! I forgot every word of my well-memorized speech.

My knees knocked, my hands shook, and my voice quivered. I prayed, "God, give me back my speech."

The crowd sat in intense silence while I shuffled my five pages of handwritten notes. None of it made any sense.

I looked up with a nervous smile. All those eyes stared back at me. My faced turned red. I said, "Thank you," grabbed my notes, and ran off stage.

Later that day, one of the speakers told me, "Your speech was pretty good until you lost it." I felt awful.

Although it has been said that public speaking is the number one fear next to death, the real fear is not of public speaking, but of losing your place, looking stupid, being judged, and not being liked. These four common fears manifest themselves with shaky hands, quivering voice, or an upset stomach.

Many speakers experience anxiety before they speak because they don't know what to say, how to say it, where to go to say it, or how to craft a presentation. They have no system.

When I stepped off the stage that day in humiliation, I knew if I ever wanted to speak again I needed to learn how to do it right. For over thirty years I took classes, hired mentors, practiced my skills on numerous stages, and developed a powerful, proven, duplicatable system that creates a persuasive presentation and conquers fear. Later in this book, I will teach you this system.

5

The Five Speeches Every Business Owner Needs

When you speak your business, your words will draw people to you like a magnet.
--Arvee Robinson

Every business owner needs three speeches to grow their business, elevator speech, self-introduction, signature talk.

The elevator speech is a one-on-one casual encounter that answers the question, "What do you do?" in a specific way that creates interest and an immediate response.

The self-introduction, done right, is a 25- to 30-second memorable, magnetic statement that, when presented to a group, draws them to talk to you and ask for more information.

The signature talk is a scheduled five- to 90-minute presentation that sets you apart from everyone else in the room. You are the expert, not another member or guest. If done right, you will generate hot leads and attract new business.

Elevator Speech

Networking meetings are all about meeting new people and finding out what they do. When was the last time you perked up when you listened to someone's spiel? It doesn't happen often. Most business owners don't know how to capture their listeners' interest. Instead, they repeat the same boring message that never gets them business. They don't know how to get to the core of what they do, understand what their potential clients want, or develop a message that becomes an instant client magnet.

Your core message is the essence of what you do for your customers and clients. In business, this message is called an elevator speech because it takes about 30 seconds to say what you do, about the same amount of time it takes to travel from one floor to another on an elevator. The purpose of this core message is to answer the question, "What do you do?" in a way that makes your listener want to know more and ask, "How do you do that?"

Before you begin to construct your elevator pitch, choose one of the three basic desires, more money, better relationships, or vibrant health, which your products or services solve. It is important to keep your message simple. Don't use all three or you will defuse your message and confuse your audience.

When someone asks you what you do, they are thinking, "How is what you do relevant to what I need?" To answer this underlying question, in your elevator speech share the target market you serve, what you do for them, and the benefits they receive.

The Target Market You Serve

Select your target market, your ideal clients, the people you most want to work with. You want your listener to think to themselves, "That's me." or "I want that to be me." Your target is never everybody.

Be careful who you choose.

When I first started my business, I worked with a mentor who suggested that I select high-level CPA's and attorneys as my target market because I worked with them in my corporate career.

This sounded right. I marketed to them and got them to sign up as clients. Before long, I noticed they didn't respect my time or my process. They would cancel appointments and make me wait in their lobbies. I was right back in the Corporate America I escaped. I didn't like it and switched to small business owners and entrepreneurs. I've been enjoying working with them ever since.

One of my clients, Jason Christopher, went to the other extreme. A new financial planner with a big heart, he wanted to help the broke and broken, so guess what he soon became. Broke and broken. When Jason came to me for help, we quickly changed his target to a more affluent market.

The lesson here is: Be careful who you choose to work with because you could become them.

Start with the demographics you resonate with, like gender, age, career, education, and hobbies. Next, select your basic market, such as women entrepreneurs, single moms, or baby boomers. Then be creative. Sexy it up to make it sound attractive.

For example: Women entrepreneurs looking to grow their business, single moms struggling to raise small children, or baby boomers looking for a new challenge. The more specific you are, the faster you attract clients. Or you can simply add a clarifying adjective in front, such as busy, high-achieving, or top-producing.

What You Do for Them

Make a list of what you do for your clients and how you do it. For example, I teach business owners how to use public speaking to market themselves, to become a persuasive speaker, and to create money-making workshops. I do it my speaker training workshops, mastermind programs, and private coaching.

When you build your elevator speech, focus on what you do, not how you do it.

The Benefits They Receive

On a blank sheet of paper draw a "T" across the top with a line down the middle of the page. On the top left side, write the word "features" and on the top right side, write the word "benefits." Write the features of what you do in the left column and the benefits in the right. Then pick the most important feature on the left side and circle it. Next, choose two or three of the most beneficial benefits on the right side and circle them. The feature circled on the left side becomes your "what" and the three items circled on the right are your benefits. Let's put it together using my magnetic formula below:

The magnetic formula:

I + (action verb) + (target market) + (what) so they can (benefits)

Six steps to create a magnetic elevator speech:

1) Start with the word "I." You will be tempted to use "we" when you speak to individuals to give them a sense that you are part of a bigger company. This creates a disconnect because the person in front of you asked

what YOU do, not what your company does. Keep it simple and answer their question, "What do YOU do?"

2) Use a strong action verb after "I." Select an action verb that you like, for example, provide, teach, coach, empower, assist, show, educate, or work. Do not use the word "help" because everyone else uses it and it reduces you to the role of helper rather than elevate you to the role of mentor.

3) Write down the target market you chose. As discussed above, the clearer you are, the easier it is to attract your ideal client.

4) Describe what you do for your target market. This statement goes with the action verb. If you said you teach, what do you teach? If you said show, what do you show them? Keep in mind people love numbers, systems, and strategies.

5) Add **so they can . . .**

6) Insert the benefits you chose above.

Be careful with the language you use.

Use vivid words to create a picture in the mind of the listener. For example, the word "house" evokes a structure with four walls and an A-style roof. Not exciting. When you change the word "house" to the word "home," your word picture comes alive! The four-wall structure now has windows with curtains, a brick chimney with smoke pouring out, and children playing on the green grass yard with their new puppy as the sun beats gently on their cheeks.

Speak to your audience as if they are unfamiliar with your business. Refrain from using industry jargon and thousand-dollar words that make your listener feel stupid. Use simple language an 11-year-old child can understand. Easy-to-understand words will penetrate the hearts of your listeners and create instant interest.

Avoid overused words that have lost their meaning. A popular word in the 1980s was "paradigm shift." For years, it was used to describe changes in the patterns of business, mindset, and structure. It was used so much that it lost its meaning. A popular phase today is, "Take your business to the next level!" This is a meaningless generality. It's more effective to say, "Our company will take your business to six-figures in six months." We can measure this specific goal.

You are now ready to create your own magnetic core message. Here are a few examples:

"I teach people five secrets of equity and finance, **so they can** *leverage other people's money and hang on to more of their own."*

"I provide small businesses with creative solutions, **so they can** *save money and develop stronger relationships with their employees."*

Turn Your Elevator Speech into a Powerful Self-Introduction

Your elevator speech can be used in many ways, inlcuding on your website, bio, and self-introduction. Your self-introduction is what you use when you are asked to introduce yourself at a networking function. You can repurpose your core message by adding three elements.

Three simple elements to turn your elevator speech into a magnetic self-introduction:

1) Elevator speech

2) Name, company, credentials

* Wild card (add anything extra here, such as "a good referral for me is....")

3) Memorable statement: A rhythmic phrase you say at the end of your self-introduction that your audience will remember.

Example:

"I teach business owners and entrepreneurs how to use public speaking as a marketing strategy so they can attract more clients, generate unlimited leads, grow their business, and get their message out to the world. My name is Arvee Robinson, I'm the master speaker trainer, international speaker, and author, and remember, if you can't say it, you can't sell it!"

The Signature Speech

Your signature talk is the most powerful of these speeches. When crafted with precision, it is the centerpiece of public speaking, the only marketing strategy you will ever need to grow your business. We will cover it in detail in Part II.

Five-minute Business Showcase

In business networking meetings, it is getting harder and harder to get thirty minutes or more to do your signature talk. Therefore, you need to have a five- to ten-minute version of your talk ready to go. At the end of Part II, I will teach how to condense my 10-step speaker system to fit into a much shorter speech.

Thirty-Second Video Promo

Video marketing is hot these days. You, as a business owner, must know how to deliver your message in a video format, which is different from speaking to a live audience. You will learn this format at the end of Part II.

6

How to Discover Your Unique Speaking Topic, Title, and Purpose

Create a powerful title that makes people want to hear you speak.
--Arvee Robinson

My big break! I shared my first big stage with seven powerful speakers, my chance to shine from the platform. My speech, about how you can use networking to build relationships, attract prospects and generate leads, was ready to go.

The audience was with me. They laughed at every joke I told and responded to every high-five command I gave. I was excited to make a dramatic difference for these people.

I went into my close and I thought, "I got them, right where I want them, they will love my coaching program." I delivered my best close ever. I told them to go to the back of the room and

I marched with confidence down the center aisle, turned and looked back.

They sat there motionless. I waited. A couple of people on the side stood up and walked out of the room. Others got up and meandered around the room, chatting. Nobody bought.

I was stunned. What on earth did I do wrong?

I stewed about it for over a week until my next coaching call with my mentor, Eric Lofholm.

I told him what had happened. "What were you selling?" Eric asked.

"My speech coaching program." I replied.

"And what was your speech about?" he asked.

"Networking." I said.

There was a long pause on the other end of the line.

"Let me get this straight. Your speech was about networking and you sold a speaking coaching program. Is that right?"

"Yes, that's right." I replied.

"Don't you see the disconnect? They wanted to take networking information home with them. They didn't care about speech coaching. You didn't even mention it in your speech."

I didn't know what to say.

"It's simple," Eric said. "You confused your audience. And confused people don't buy."

Wow! What a breakthrough. I hadn't aligned my offer with my speech topic. Duh! I never made that mistake again.

Why? I offered speech coaching because I wanted to sell speech coaching, not the networking product I had created for this event.

I was confused. I love coaching speakers. My program was ideal for it. And I was going to give my networking program for free for signing up for my speech coaching program. That should take care of it. Eric's words echoed in my mind. And then it hit me. The problem was that I had given the wrong speech, not sold the wrong product. My unique speaking topic was about speaking, not networking.

I let the promoters of the seminar dictate the subject of my speech because I thought I could sell speech coaching with any speech no matter what topic. Eric showed me how wrong I was.

If I wanted to sell speech coaching, I had to create a signature talk that emphasized my unique topic of how to use public speaking as a marketing strategy and give it every time I spoke.

Since then, my signature talk, *Speak Up, Cash In: How to Use Public Speaking as a Marketing Strategy to Attract High-paying Clients*, is the only speech I give.

And guess what? People buy.

How to Discover Your Unique Speaking Topic

One of the biggest reasons business owners have trouble selecting a topic is that their business has so many aspects it is difficult to choose one.

For example, my business is public speaking coaching and training. I could talk about closing sales, hand gestures, speakers as leaders, seminars, and so forth. Because my passion is working with business owners and entrepreneurs, I chose public speaking as a marketing strategy as my unique topic.

To discover your unique subject, ask yourself these questions:

- What do I know?
- What part am I passionate about?
- What problems do I solve?
- Who do I solve these problems for?
- How do I transform businesses?
- How do I change people's lives?

- What are my unique gifts?
- How do I share these gifts with others?

The answers will guide you to your unique speaking topic.

Once you've zeroed in on your unique speaking topic and before you write a word of your speech, create your title.

What do I call my signature talk?

The minute I saw the title, I knew the audience was in trouble.

My friend Linda Cain scheduled me to speak to a group of mediators. Whenever I don't know much about an organization, I make it a point to visit one of their meetings in advance. Linda and I fought through traffic to get to the Santa Monica Library for this meeting.

We walked into a crowded room and sat down. After we introduced ourselves to the people at our table I glanced up at the screen and gasped. The title read, *101 Ways to Market Your Mediation Business.*

"We're in trouble," I whispered to Linda.

The speaker proceeded to rattle off a bunch of headlines like a machine gun but had no time to drill down deep with any one idea.

Halfway through his speech, I looked around. People were yawning, playing with their cell phones, doodling on papers. They were bored to tears!

After 90 minutes, a voice came over the loud speaker, "The library will close in five minutes." Instead of wrapping up his speech and going into his close, he spoke faster and faster until the host stepped onto the stage and dragged him off. I'm sure he had a lot of knowledge to share, he shouldn't have shared it all at once. His title doomed his speech for several reasons:

- It's impossible to speak in depth on that many points in the time allotted.

- He bored the audience with an endless laundry list of information.
- He had no time for stories or audience interaction.
- He ran out of time long before he ran out of speech and was dragged off the stage.
- He had no opportunity to sell his book or talk to audience members to see if they wanted to become clients after the speech.

Audiences show up at meetings because the speaker's speech title and topic attract them. Make yours benefit driven, inviting, and customized to what that specific audience wants.

Use either numbers, secrets, or "how to" in the title to create anticipation.

Numbers imply a step-by-step system. The word "secrets" creates curiosity. How-to titles mean the speaker will train instead of talk.

Here are seven examples of successful speech titles:

- Seven Secrets to Creating a Persuasive Presentation That Sells
- Five Easy Ways to Eliminate Stage Fright Forever
- Top Ten Tips You Can Use to Keep Your Man Happy
- How to Negotiate Like a Pro and Create Win-Win Deals
- How to Convert Your Audience from Listeners into Hungry Buyers
- What the Surgeons Don't Want You to Know about Plastic Surgery
- The Most Common Tax Mistake You're Making Now

Now that you have your subject and title, get clear on your purpose for speaking, who your audience is, what you are going to give them, and what you want them to do with this information. This is your *purpose statement*.

The Purpose Statement

A purpose statement defines your speech but is not included in it.

A purpose statement is your private roadmap to your speech's destination. It answers these questions:

What is your main purpose for speaking?

Who are you speaking to?

What value are you giving?

What action do you want your audience to take?

Although it is the key element in developing your speech, it never appears in your speech. It is for your personal use only. Create a separate purpose statement for each speech you develop.

To create yours, follow this simple formula:

Purpose + Audience + Value + Action (PAVA) = Purpose statement.

Purpose. There are six basic reasons for speaking, from least to most effective. Trained speakers use more than one of these, but not all of them, in their speeches:

- Inform (give basic information)
- Entertain (feel good, no usable value)
- Educate (give usable information, no action)
- Motivate (rah, rah words without lasting value)
- Inspire (change mindset to want positive action)
- Persuade (decision to take specific action)

Many untrained business speakers fill their speech with boring information about their business, their products, who they are, and where they came from. Then they sit down. The audience thinks, "That was a lot of information," and forgets what they heard.

This happens because they use the least effective of the six basic purposes as the primary purpose of their speech, to inform. Even worse, they use none of the other five purposes in their speech.

Trained business speakers speak on stage to generate leads, attract clients, and close sales. As their primary purpose, they use persuade, the most effective of the six basic purposes, to get their audience to take specific action at the end of their speech.

To make their speech even more effective, they also use one or more of the other purposes, such as inspire, educate, or motivate, as needed to fulfill their primary purpose.

Audience. If your target market is business owners, remember that there are many types of businesses. You need to know whether you are speaking to accountants or life coaches because each group has its own wants, needs, and desires. Use that specific group when you write your purpose statement.

Value. The title of your speech reflects the value you bring to your audience. Insert if here.

Action. What action do you want your audience to take at the end of your presentation? Five possible actions your audience could take are:

- **Give you their business card**. Raffle off a free gift and in return gather everyone's contact information and build your database.
- **Sign up for free services**. Offer a free 30-minute session over the phone or in person. This gives you the opportunity to close the sale.
- **Ask questions**. Invite them to ask you questions after your talk. The people most interested in your products and services will respond and become hot leads.
- **Give referrals**. Pass out forms and ask for contact information on anyone who could use your products or services. It also works to get speaking engagements.
- **Buy a product or service at the end of your presentation**. Sell from the platform and close sales.

Choose the action that best suits your business and speech.

Example of purpose statements:

Formula: Purpose + Audience + Value + Action (PAVA) = Purpose statement

- Persuade + local business owners + five secrets to financial freedom + give me their contact information
- Persuade + corporate sales team + objection handling tips + sign up for a free 30-minute coaching session
- Persuade + coaches and consultants + to write and publish a book that attracts new clients + give me referrals of new coaches and consultants

You can also write it out in a complete sentence:

To *persuade* local business owners by sharing five secrets to financial freedom so they will give me their business card at the end of my speech.

To *persuade* a corporate sales team by teaching objection handling tips so they will want to sign up for a free 30-minute coaching session.

To *persuade* coaches and consultants to write and publish a book that attracts new clients, so they will give me referrals of other new coaches and consultants who need business.

Your purpose statement keeps you focused on what you want to give and what you want to receive. Every point you make during your speech serves this primary purpose. This road map prevents you from traveling off course.

Now that you've laid the foundation, it's time to craft your persuasive presentation.

Part II

The System:
How to Craft Your Sales-
winning, Life-changing,
Memorable Signature
Speech!

7

The Speech Sandwich

Once you know the type of speech you plan to deliver, writing it is as easy as making a sandwich.
--Arvee Robinson

When I was five years old, my mom would make me baloney sandwiches. She always used two pieces of bread, with a little mayonnaise and a slice of baloney in the middle.

I loved them!

Build your speech like my mom built my sandwich.

Your speech must have a beginning, middle, and end. Using the sandwich metaphor, the first slice of bread is your rapport builder, the beginning of your talk. It has five components: attention grabber, welcome, thank yous, summary, and your professional story.

The meat of your presentation is your knowledge, what the audience came to hear. If it's not in the rapport builder or close, it goes in the meat.

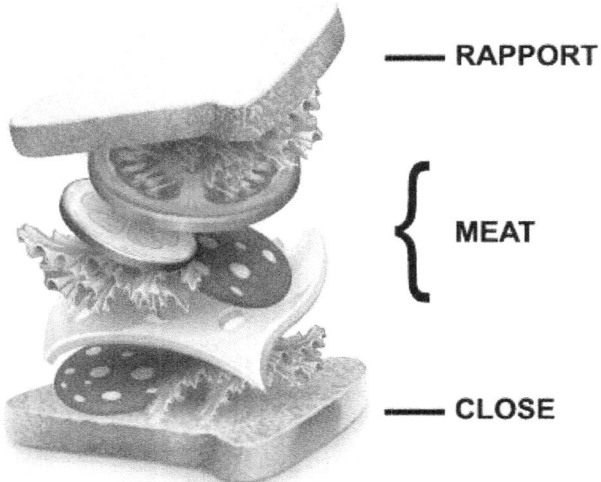

Add stories, quotes and audience participation to spice up the meat. These spices are similar to the tomato, onion, avocado, and lettuce you would add to your own sandwich.

My mom dressed up her baloney sandwiches with mayonnaise, which is why they tasted so good. You dress up your speech when you connect your solution to your audience's problems, which is why your speech tastes so good.

Be creative when you spice up your sandwich. No one wants to eat a dry sandwich or listen to a boring speech.

The bottom slice of bread represents the end of your talk: the close. Here, you invite your audience to take the next step with you, either set up an appointment, sign up for a free coaching session, or buy on the spot.

Like the top piece of bread, the close also consists of five major steps: summary, question and answer, invitation, thanking your audience, and a memorable statement.

If you make a sandwich with only the top piece of bread, it falls apart. In many business presentations, the speaker begins with valuable information and ends without a close. The speech falls apart and no one buys.

Both pieces of bread are equal in size (five steps each). The meat in the middle may vary depending on the time you have to speak. No matter how short or long your speech is, you never eliminate the bread. Instead you reduce the meat and spices. It's better to spice up one piece of information than cram too much into too little time.

Now that you know the basic elements of a well-crafted speech, it's time to learn each step in my *Million Dollar Speaker System*™ so you can create your own tasty speech. (See Appendix 10 for full graphic representation).

8

How to Build Rapport with Your Audience

The key to platform success is the ability to make your audience feel loved.

--Arvee Robinson

Step 1: Grab Your Audience's Attention

I wanted to scream.

I had finished eating the veggie omelet at my favorite chamber breakfast meeting when the guest speaker was introduced.

His first words were, "Good morning. We have 15 offices around the United States."

I gasped. Another boring business presentation.

As a speaker, you have three seconds to grab your audience's attention. In those precious seconds your audience will size you up and decide whether you will bore them or interest them. It happens that fast.

Three effective ways to grab your audience's attention are:

Enrolling Questions

I start my presentations with enrolling questions because they engage both the audience's mind and body. When you ask your audience benefit-driven questions, their brains want an answer.

A way to engage the body is to raise your hand as you ask the questions. Your audience will raise their hand too.

Base your questions on what your specific audience wants.

For example, I begin many of my talks with this question:

"How many of you want to attract more clients?"

Raise your right hand when you ask the first question. This encourages your audience to raise their right hand. If they don't, add, "By a show of hands."

The second question builds on the first. Raise your left hand, repeat the first question and add another benefit. For example:

"How many of you not only want to attract more clients, you want to do it today?"

Or you could build like this:

"How many of you want to attract more clients?"

"How many of you want to attract a lot more clients?"

Repetition creates excitement. The audience can't wait to get the results you promise. One question doesn't build enough excitement and three kills the excitement.

Statistical Statements

A few months after I started my business, I was shocked when the speaker at my local Chamber of Commerce luncheon said, *"Eighty-five percent of all small businesses go out of business within the first five years!"*

I didn't want to be a statistic. From that moment, the speaker had my undivided attention.

He used a powerful way to start his speech, "statistical statements," which features staggering percentages or numbers.

If this speaker had said, *"Thirty percent of all small businesses go out of business in the first five years,"* I would not have been shocked. If there's a better than 70% chance of starting a successful company, why mention it? It's not news.

When you use a statistical statement, make it greater than 50% or nobody will care. To make your statement even more believable, use odd numbers and decimal points. For example, *"83.5 percent of all small businesses go out of business within the first five years!"*

Statistical statements work best when the speaker is a lawyer, accountant, financial advisor, insurance broker, banker, or health professional. These scary statistics shock the audience members into listening because they don't want to become that statistic.

Every number you use must be correct and current. Always get your stats from reliable sources so you can respond if an expert in the audience challenges you.

Dramatic Declarations

A dramatic declaration is a powerful, emotional statement based on the speaker's truth and experience, not the audience's. For instance, a health coach will say, "I have an amazing body!" Now everyone in the audience wants to know how the speaker got that amazing body.

Quotes, Jokes and Stories

"I like to start my speech with a joke," the speaker announced. The audience let out a loud sigh.

One of the fastest ways to lose your audience is to use jokes, quotes, or stories as an attention grabber. Here's why.

First, opening your presentation with a joke is similar to talking about your ex on the first date. It has the potential to alienate your audience and sabotage your speech before you even get started. The biggest challenge with jokes is that you don't know who they may or may not offend. It's too risky.

Starting your talk with another expert's quote is not a good idea either. "Tony Robbins says, 'Good isn't good enough, you must be outstanding!'" Who is the audience thinking about? Tony Robbins, not you!

Using a story to start your speech is also dangerous. It is the exact opposite of an attention-grabbing statement. Since a story is longer, slower and far less dramatic, it deflates the audience's energy.

Even worse is making up a story.

"Before I left the airport, I bought a bag of chocolate chip cookies. I love chocolate chip cookies," the speaker began.

I listened with contempt because I knew he was lying.

How could a speaker who lived in Southern California tell a story about flying to a marketing seminar in Southern California?

"I boarded the plane, sat next to a beautiful young lady and set my bag down between the seats. She reached into it and ate one of my cookies!

"I smiled at her, reached into my bag, grabbed a cookie, and chomped. She smiled and reached into my bag and took another cookie. This went on until one cookie was left. She motioned for me to take the last cookie. I grinned and thought to myself, 'thank you for letting me have my last cookie! Instead, I gestured, 'You take it.' By then the plane had landed and I got up.

"I reached into the overhead compartment to gather my carry-on luggage. In the side pocket of my briefcase I saw a little brown bag *filled with chocolate chips cookies! Uh oh! I was eating her cookies the entire flight!"*

Everyone in the audience laughed (except me).

I've heard that story so many times I knew it didn't happen to him. He didn't even get on a plane to come to the event; he drove his car. After that, I couldn't believe a word he said. I wondered how many people in that audience had heard the story before and felt the same way.

The first three seconds are vital to the success of your speech. They set the tone for your entire presentation.

To grab your audience fast, stick to one of these three proven attention grabbers: enrolling questions, statistical statements, or dramatic declarations.

Step 2. Welcome

The second step to building rapport is short. First, to make your audience feel welcome, acknowledge their participation by saying 'great' or 'fantastic.'

Second, let them know what you are going to talk about and for how long.

For instance, if your title is: "How to Attract High-paying Clients Every Time You Speak," you could say: *"For the next 30 minutes I'm going to share with you how you can use public speaking to attract high-paying clients."*

3. Thank Your Audience

Since we are still in our rapport building phase, the fastest way to build rapport is to say, "Thank you." Rapport building must be initiated in the beginning of your talk to be effective. Most business presenters say thank you at the end of their speech and by then it is too late.

During this step, thank your audience for their time, energy, and the effort they took to hear you speak. Don't make this a simple "Thank you for being here." To build rapport you need to be real and speak in the moment. For example:

"I would like to take a moment and thank you for taking time out of your busy day to be here, I appreciate it."

Next, thank your host or the person who invited you to speak that day. Hosts love recognition and applause. Applaud them by saying, *"I would also like to thank Mary Smith, your President, for inviting me here to speak with you today. Let's give Mary a hand!"*

When you thank them, use their full name out of respect for who they are and the office they serve. Never thank the assistant in public even if that person did all the work. This disrespect for the host (or boss) could cost you future speaking engagements.

4. Summary

In this step, use your title to get permission to transition into your personal story. Using a small variation from step two to remind them of the content, you can say: *"Before I share with you how you can attract more high-paying clients every time you speak would it be okay if I shared a little bit about myself?"*

Nod your head up and down as if you are saying "yes."

The audience will nod back, giving you permission to talk about yourself. How cool is that?!

5. Professional Story

The last step in the rapport building process is a story about your journey, how you got to where you are today and why they should listen to you.

In the beginning of this book, I shared my professional story of how I got into public speaking, which led me to where I am today, an international speaker and master speaker trainer who wants to help you get on more stages and make a ton of money.

Your professional story is the quickest way to gain credibility, build rapport with your audience, and earn the right to speak on your topic. This leads the audience to know you, like you, trust you, and want to buy from you.

First, your professional story must be relevant to your topic, audience, and what you're selling. For instance, if your topic is writing skills don't talk about how you became a financial planner. If your audience is stay-at-home moms don't talk about why you never had children. If you are talking about networking don't sell speech coaching.

Second, talk about the journey that led you to where you are today. The story starts when an unexpected event forces you out of your normal situation and into a challenge you must overcome. This is the turning point that defines you and creates your new destiny.

Think of this story as going from a mess to success. We've all heard stories about people becoming a millionaire, losing it all, and then becoming a millionaire again. People love rags to riches stories because they show it is possible for them to succeed too. When you show the audience you were where they are now, they will connect with you at a deeper level.

To connect at this level, you must understand your deepest emotions and use those feelings and experiences to add depth to the way you tell your story. When you talk about a happy moment, show your happiness. When you share a moment of despair, show your emotions. Use your voice, tone, physical actions and facial expressions to create the moment. Don't over emote or under emote. Be vulnerable, be yourself, and be real.

Third, your professional story should be relevant to your topic. It is not a chronological re-telling of your life history. It is a story that shows your specific journey to how you came to do what you do and why you are talking about it today. Your story will vary in length depending on how long you are speaking.

As a guideline, in a one-hour talk, your story should be no more than five to seven minutes.

When you tell your story the right way, it will open the hearts of your listeners. When their hearts open, their wallets open.

To start your story, think back to when you were a child. Do you remember how those folk tales, fairy tales and tall tales began?

"Once upon a time, deep in the heart of the forest...."

"Long, long, ago in a small village in England...."

Start with a time and place to relax your audience. They will lower their guard and snuggle up for a delightful story.

For example, I start my story with:

"I spent 23 years (time) in Corporate America (place)."

Or

"In 1982 (time), I worked for an International CPA firm in downtown Los Angeles (place)."

If you remember your folk tales, life is great and then BOOM, an unexpected event happens.

To reveal your unexpected event, begin your next statement with, "One day..." and then share the unexpected event that led you to where you are today.

"One day, the wicked witch cast an evil spell..."

You can have more than one unexpected event. The first unexpected event that changed my life started when a woman came up to me at the end of my talk and told me that I said *okay* after every sentence. My second was the effect of 911 on my career. What are your unexpected events?

Show your story, don't tell it. Most speakers make the mistake of telling their story without visual detail or scene. It lacks immediacy and emotion. Your audience yawns through it. To grab their attention with your story, use vivid scenes they can visualize, specific quoted dialogue, and telling details that create a deep emotional experience in your listeners minds.

An example of telling a story is the following:

My son hadn't come home all day. I was worried. Then the phone rang, the policeman was on the line. He told me there had been an accident. I got even more worried. He told me to go to the hospital, so I raced to the hospital.

To show this story:

Four o'clock in the afternoon. My seven-year-old son still hadn't come home. "Where could he be," I thought. The next ten minutes felt like an hour. I paced and paced. The phone rang! I hesitated, then ran to pick it up. "Yes?" I said and held my breath.

"This is Captain Jones down at the police station. Are you Mrs. Smith?" My heart sank. "I am."

"There's been an accident." Captain Jones said. "Your son was hit by a car and is in the hospital. You need to get down there now."

I grabbed my purse, checked to see that the keys were in it and ran out the door. I hit every red light on the way to the hospital and ran into the emergency room breathless with anticipation and dread.

As you can see, a shown story evokes deep emotions and makes your audience experience your story with you.

To finish your story, tell them the lesson you learned from your experience, what you are doing now as a result, and how they can do it too.

For example, at the end of my story I say, *"I left the corporate world and started my own business. Since then I've taught people all over the world how to use public speaking as a marketing strategy to attract more clients, generate unlimited leads, and grow their businesses fast."*

When you use the right ingredients in the right order in this last step in the rapport building section of the speech sandwich, you will generate the audience rapport needed to create a solid foundation for the rest of your speech.

9

The Flavor is in the Dressing

Dress up your speech like you would for a night on the town.
--Arvee Robinson

Using my speech sandwich metaphor, if you were to create a sandwich without mayonnaise or other dressing, your sandwich would be dry. It's the moist flavor of dressing that gets our palate ready to savor the meat.

Your speech works the same way. The dressing touches your audience's emotional center, where all the buying decisions are made, and sets the table for a successful speech.

The PPS statement (problem, pain and suffering, solution) is the dressing, the secret sauce.

State the PPS

To develop your PPS statement, answer these questions:
What is the biggest problem my clients or customers face?
What pain and suffering does the problem cause?
How am I the solution to the problem?

For example, my PPS is:

Problem

Most business owners are afraid to speak in front of groups, because they don't know what to say, how to say it, or where to say it. They give up before they even try.

Pain and suffering

They don't realize that by not speaking, they are losing a ton of business and missing out on helping more people. This could cost them their business.

It doesn't have to be this way!

Solution

"I teach business owners a step-by-step speaking system so they can create a persuasive business presentation guaranteed to attract more clients, generate unlimited leads, and grow their businesses fast."

When your audience hears your solution, they salivate because they can't wait to bite into your juicy sandwich.

Honesty is the key that makes the secret sauce tasty. Show them you understand how much it will cost them in the long run if they don't solve their problem.

Then BE the solution.

10

The Meat is in the Middle (Make it Tasty)

Memorize the beginning and end of your speech and let your knowledge flow in the middle.
--Arvee Robinson

Now we move into the content of your speech, the meat. This is your knowledge, your gifts, the golden nuggets of information you give your audience.

The secret sauce allows you to make a smooth transition into the meat of your speech.

When deciding how much meat to add to your sandwich you need to know how much time you have to speak.

If you try to cover too many points in too short a time, it's like making a sandwich that is stacked so high with meat that no one can bite into it. On the other hand, if you have more time after you deliver what you promised, give your audience a bonus slice.

55

Earlier, I mentioned the speaker whose title was *101 Ways to Market Your Mediation Business*. He created a sandwich that was so big no-one could get their teeth around it. They tuned out. He was still speaking when a voice came over the loudspeaker announcing the Library was closing in five minutes. He kept talking. Then a security guard told us all to leave. He kept talking. Then the organizer pulled him off the stage. He was still talking as he walked out of building. In his effort to get all of his information in, he missed his opportunity to close and forfeited potential sales.

Don't let this happen to you.

You choose how much meat to put into your speech sandwich based on how much time you have to speak:

- 5- to 7-minute speech = 1 piece of meat or information
- 20- to 30-minute speech = 3 pieces of meat
- 35- to 45-minute speech = 5 pieces of meat
- 50- to 60-minute speech = 7 pieces of meat
- 60- to 90-minute speech = 10 pieces of meat

These guidelines will allow you to go deep enough into each point and still keep your audience craving more.

In Chapter 5 you selected your ultimate topic, developed your purpose statement, and created your sizzling benefit driven title.

If your title is *Five Ways to Attract High-paying Clients with Public Speaking,* you will have five pieces of meat, or main points, in your talk.

Next, outline your content. Do not write out your speech. If you do, you will be imprisoned by the words you write. You will have a burning desire to memorize it and read it from your memory. This leads to robotic delivery and all too often your speech will vanish from your memory at the wrong moment. I've seen this happen time and time again.

True freedom of expression is achieved when you are free to speak your knowledge and not be tied to a script. An outline gives your speech a basic structure and keeps you focused. It gives you the freedom to say what you want, when you want, and the flexibility to interact with your audience.

Here is an example of one of my outlines:

Title: *Five Ways to Attract High-paying Clients with Public Speaking*.

1. You can reach more people at once
2. Positions you as an expert in your field
3. People get to know you
4. Build your database fast
5. Attract hot sizzling leads

You could also use an acronym for the same five points. An acronym is a word that includes the first letter of each of your main points and is used as a memory tool to remind you of your key points. For the audience, it creates curiosity and is a fun way to learn. You can use them out of order if you make it clear which point you are talking about. Here is an example:

L - Leverage, you can reach more people at once

E - Expert, it positions you as an expert in your field

A - Audience, people get to know you

D - Database, you can build your database fast

S - Sizzling leads, attract hot leads every time you speak

You can add quotes, examples, demonstrations, or audience exercises and breakouts to your meat to spice it up.

Stories are the most flavorful spices and will captivate your audience. Decide what stories you want to tell and add them to your outline. In the next chapter, we will cover the four stories you must include your speeches.

11

Captivate Your Listeners with Stories

To become a great salesperson, you must become a great storyteller.

--Arvee Robinson

Once upon a time in a village long, long, ago there was a beautiful princess . . .

People have been captivating audiences with folk tales, fairy tales, and tall tales for centuries. History has been passed from generation to generation with stories. Lives have been transformed by telling a story. While these are compelling reasons to use stories in your presentation, the number one reason is that stories hold the key to persuasion and influence. We've all heard that "facts tell and stories sell!"

My mentor, Eric Lofholm, Master Sales Trainer, says, "Stories act as invisible selling."

Stories sell because they speak to the subconscious mind, where they create a powerful emotional response that opens the listener's heart. Once the heart is open the pocketbook flies open.

These four types of stories will add emotional power to your presentation:

1. Professional story
2. Success stories
3. Emotional stories
4. Lesson stories

Professional story

Your professional story builds rapport with your audience and earns you the right to speak. No matter how much or how little time you have to speak, always include it.

Success stories

Nothing sells faster than success.

Success stories share the results one of your clients or customers achieves after working with you. It's a form of bragging without blowing your own horn, similar to a third-party endorsement or a testimonial.

Your audience will experience your success through the story and understand how your programs will create success in their business.

One of my favorite success stories is about Hector Gonzales, a successful photographer. His dream was to be a sales trainer and teach the Hispanic market in Spanish how to create more sales. He started speaking to his target market and failed. He came to me, I taught him my speaking system, and the next time he spoke he sold $7,500 in a 30-minute talk. Now he can use these skills to make money and help others for the rest of his life.

Throughout this book, I've shared many client success stories. Jill learned to overcome the fear of speaking, Donavan closed so many sales he bought a yacht, and Pete the Accountant was so entertaining that he closed eight new tax clients.

Emotional stories

An emotional story can get your audience to cry like a baby or it could make them laugh.

One Sunday morning, the church pastor noticed a young boy about nine years old gazing up at the wall. The boy was studying the black and white pictures hanging there.

"Young man, did you know that those are men who died in the service?" the pastor asked. The boy looked up at him and asked, "Was it the 9 o'clock service or the 10 o'clock service?"

Humor is always the easiest and safest emotion to elicit during your speech. As the old saying goes, "Funny equals money!"

Lesson stories

I learned the following story from one of my mentors and often tell it during my live seminars.

How many great cooks do we have in the audience?

This is a story about a great cook.

One day her husband watched her cook a roast. She took the roast out of the refrigerator and cut the ends off. Her husband asked her, "Why do you do that?"

She shrugged and replied, "I don't know, that's the way my mom taught me."

The husband, not happy with the answer said, "We're going to call mom and get to the bottom of this."

The husband picked up the phone and called mom. When mom answered the phone, the son-in-law said, "Mom, I have your daughter here and every time she cooks a roast she cuts off the ends. Why did you teach her to do it that way?"

Mom replied, "I don't know, that's how my mom taught me."

Now frustrated, the husband told mom to hang on while he dialed grandma to have a three-way conversation.

Grandma answered the phone.

The husband said, "Grandma, I have your daughter and your granddaughter on the phone and they both cut the ends of the roast off before they cook it. Why did you teach them to do it that way?"

Grandma laughed and said, "When I was younger the ovens were much smaller. We had to cut off the ends to fit it in the oven!"

So, I ask you what are you doing in your business today because that is the way you've always done it? Mark Victor Hansen says 95% of what we do is out of habit.

Perhaps it's time to change old habits.

This emotional story also includes a lesson: We tend to act out of habit and don't always know why.

You can teach the lesson as in the example above or you could hide in a metaphor.

In 2010, I was thrilled to be asked to be a mentor for Chris Howard's Billionaire Adventure Club, an eight-day excursion to Egypt. I was one of 19 mentors working with 100 professionals who traveled from all over the world to be there. What a fantastic opportunity!

A small group, 23 of us, decided to take the post trip and see the sun rise over Mount Sinai. If you know your Bible history, you'll know that Mount Sinai is where Moses was handed the Ten Commandments.

The bus dropped us off at the base of Saint Catherine's Monastery at 2 a.m. The famous burning bush grows on a hill above the courtyard at St. Catherine's Church (no it's not burning any more).

I heard 2,000 people per day climb this mountain like ants scurrying up a big anthill.

There are two ways to climb to the top of Mount Sinai. One is to climb 3,750 steps; the other is to ride a camel. I did what any smart woman would do, I rode a camel.

I've never been on a camel before, so I had no idea what to expect. After waiting a few minutes, one of the Bedouin, the native cave dwellers, grabbed me and sat me on his kneeling camel. An instant later, the Bedouin whacked the camel's behind and up went the camel's rear end. All of a sudden, I'm sitting on a steep slope struggling to hang on, staring at the desert sand below me. Then the front end went up and now I'm sitting 13 feet in the air holding on for dear life!

My camel proceeded to follow other camels up a narrow trail with the mountain on one side and a drop off on the other. The camel owner walked alongside chanting what sounded like, "Mar-dy, Mar-dy!" We rode higher up the mountain. My camel began meandering from one side of the path to the other. The owner's mantra became louder, "Mar-dy, Mar-dy," until I couldn't take it anymore.

Imagine this, it's pitch black, there's a cliff a couple of feet away and you can't hear a sound, except me screaming, "Oh - My - God!"

A nearby Bedouin said, "Don't worry Madam, the camel knows the way." At that moment I realized, it's not the camel's first time, it's my first time!

I relaxed and let the camel lead the way up Mount Sinai. We went as far as the camels could take us and climbed another 750 steps to the top.

I sat on big boulders with thousands of people, all waiting in silence for the sun to rise.

When the orange glow of the sun peeked out from across the horizon, the Bedouin began to sing. In that breathtaking moment, I felt closer to God than ever, like I could touch the heavens.

If I hadn't pushed through the fear, I wouldn't have had this amazing experience or this inspirational story to tell.

The real life-lesson of this story is when you trust the system, no matter how scary it seems, you'll be safe. You will conquer your fear. In Egypt I trusted their system in every scary situation I faced and survived them all. When you trust my speaking system, even though you may be afraid of speaking, you will succeed.

12

The Close That Gets Your Audience Off Their Duff

*When selling from the stage, practice your close
more than the entire rest of your speech.*
--Arvee Robinson

The biggest mistake I see untrained speakers make is no call to action. No close.

Think about it. If you make a sandwich and forget the bottom piece of bread, what happens to your sandwich? It falls apart. That is what happens to a speech when the presenter forgets the close.

Without the close, you will get no business.

While at a business networking event, I introduced myself to a young gentleman standing nearby.

"I gave a speech yesterday!" He said with pride.

"Wonderful!" I said. "How many clients did you get?"

"Ah, none." He answered.

65

"How many leads did you generate?" I asked.

"Ah, none." He replied.

It doesn't matter how good a speaker you are, at the end of the speech all that matters is how many leads you generated.

The results are in the close. Without the close, save your breath, time and effort and don't speak at all. You must learn how to close.

Using the "Speech Sandwich" metaphor, the final piece of bread is called *The Close*. This is where you ask for the business. The Close contains five steps: Summary, question and answer (Q & A), invitation (call to action), thank you, and a memorable statement. It is crucial to execute each step in the proper order.

Let's take a closer look at how each step gets your audience ready to jump up scream, "I want to work with you!"

1. Summary

Restate the title of your talk the way you did in step two and step four but in the past tense:

"That Ladies and Gentlemen is *how you can attract high-paying clients every time you speak!*"

That's all you need to say to transition to the next step, your Question and Answer. This summary sentence can be your speech title word for word or you can paraphrase it. Its sole purpose is to let your audience know you have completed the content (the meat) and you're moving into your close.

2. Question and Answer Session

Now let's take a moment and talk about your question and answer session (Q and A) and whether or not it is necessary.

Conducting a Q and A session at the end of your talk is an old model of speaking. In the old days, a speaker would deliver 30 minutes of content and conduct a 15-minute Q and A session afterwards. If you do that today you are setting yourself up for trouble. Yes, most people in your audience have legitimate questions but a few will try to hijack your speech. These include:

- The showboat who wants to talk about themselves and never asks a real question.
- The heckler who asks you a difficult question to throw you off your speech.
- The know-it-all who wants to challenge your expertise.
- The goofball who asks stupid questions not relevant to your talk.

Either way, this is a lose-lose proposition for you as the speaker.

You also may be speaking to an involved audience that asks a lot of questions. If you are not careful, you could run out of time before you have the opportunity to invite your audience to take the next step with you, thank them, and leave them with your memorable statement.

Instead of a full-blown Q and A session, invite your audience to approach you with their questions after your presentation.

Here's the script I use:

"I know you have questions, and I want to answer them. I will be standing right here after the meeting. Please ask me any questions you like."

You've created an opportunity to receive hot leads.

Think of it this way. You have a tall haystack in front of you and you need to find the needles in the haystack. You are the magnet. When you ask your audience to see you after the meeting, you are magnet, attracting potential clients to you.

The people with valid questions who want to work with you will approach you at the end of your talk. You've eliminated the showboats, hecklers, know-it-alls and goof-balls. How cool is that?!

What you do next is important.

Several people may line up to talk to you. Because you can only take a short time with each one before the others lose interest and leave, you need to conclude each encounter fast.

When your first prospect approaches you, look him or her straight in the eye. If you don't, you will break the connection and the rapport. After you hear the question, reply by saying, "That's a great question. I'd like to spend more time than we have right now to answer it. Would it be okay if I called you tomorrow?"

After your prospect says "yes" ask for a business card so you can follow up, "Great, may I have your business card?"

The prospect often replies, "I gave you a business card during the raffle." (See step three, *The Invitation*).

"Yes, you did, however that card will go to my assistant to enter into my database. I would like another one, so I can follow up with you myself."

When your prospect hands you the business card, continue to look into his or her eyes. Without looking at it, fold the corner of the card to signify it is a hot lead. Then move on to the next person. Call each prospect within 24 hours or these hot leads will become stone cold.

For now, let's get back to the Q and A session because you say, "I want my audience to ask me questions!"

There are two exceptions to this rule. First, complex presentations warrant a Q and A session. For example, if you are an attorney speaking about reverse mortgages, living trusts, or estate planning you need a Q and A to answer the questions your presentation raises.

Second, if you are speaking in your own room, where you control the schedule, it is okay to have a Q and A session if you believe it will enhance your presentation and lead them to the close.

If you have a complex topic and feel it necessary to have a Q and A session, here is how to make it successful.

"Are there any questions?" the speaker asked.

The audience sat there. No one said a word.

"Thank you very much," the speaker said. Then he walked off the stage.

What went wrong? The audience didn't see the Q and A session coming. This awkward moment of silence can be avoided by giving your audience a minute to think of a question.

Ask: "Are there any questions?" Wait a second and if no hands are raised…say, "A typical question I hear is 'What do I wear when I speak?'"

I then say, "You dress in what's authentic for you, and what's respectful for your audience and your topic. Dress as if you are going to a job interview, wedding, or church. Always remember to dress without distractions.

"For women, a distraction could be dangling earrings, scarves, open toed shoes, or low-cut blouses. I've seen earrings so long that every time the speaker moved her head side to side they slapped her face. Ouch!

"Another distraction is too much bling jewelry or clothing. Unless you are modeling and selling this type of fashion, it's best to tone it down for your presentation.

"Inappropriate shoes or low-cut blouses can also be a huge distraction to your audience. If they are not looking at your face, chances are they're not listening to what you say.

"Same goes for men. Dress your dressiest, authentic self and always with respect for your audience. Leave the goofy animal ties at home unless you're a zoo keeper going on the David Letterman show. Be sure to take off your cell phone holster so your audience won't be distracted waiting for your phone to ring. Empty all your pockets to eliminate bulges and jingles.

"Are there any more questions?"

Were you so enthralled by this process that you forgot you were having a Q and A session? Your audience will too.

This gives your audience time to think of possible questions. They will respond one of two ways, ask a question or be silent.

If they ask a question, you answer it. If not, you go on to the next step, the invitation.

Either way they had a Q and A session.

When an audience member asks a question, first thank them, repeat the question for clarification, and then answer it to the best of your ability.

If you can't answer the question, be honest and handle it this way. "That's a good question. I don't know the answer. However, I will find it and get back to you."

Another possibility is let a participant answer it. "That's a great question. Does anyone here know the answer?"

Whatever you do don't let the question get you flustered.

When you conduct a Q and A you must control it.

Don't get off topic or let anyone in your audience take over. If this happens, say, "Great questions, however let's get back on track."

Don't let your Q and A session go too long. Remember, you need time to complete three more steps in your close. This could take up to 15 minutes depending on the type of invitation (call to action) you've selected.

To end your Q and A session, say, "We have time for one more question." or "That ends our Q and A session for today. If you have any more questions, please see me after the meeting."

This will tell your audience the Q and A portion of your presentation has ended.

Now go into your invitation.

3. The Invitation

The invitation or call to action is the most crucial step in your entire speech. This is what you have been preparing your audience for from the beginning. The rapport building steps such as the thank you, your personal story, the pain and suffering, and delivering value all lead to this one moment. The moment of truth.

Are they going to act?

During this phase, you invite your audience to act. You may be asking yourself, "Do what?" Remember your purpose statement in Chapter 5? You answered the question, "What action do you want them to take?"

There are five different actions you can ask your audience to take during this step. They are:

Invite them to participate in a raffle (business card strategy). If you have a small database (1,000 names or less), this is the strategy I recommend until you reach 3,000 names. The money is in the database. Using this strategy, you'll build your list every time you speak. Your audience will stay on your list and receive your marketing emails longer because they heard you speak.

Offer a free strategy session. Invite your audience to sign up for a free 30-minute session with you which can take place over the phone or in person. The over the phone session works best for businesses who coach and mentor individuals. The in-person session works best for businesses who need to demonstrate what they do. For example, fitness coaches could provide a 30-minute hands-on workout. Either way, this conversation will give you a chance to learn more about your prospect and how you can solve their problem.

Ask for referrals. Pass out referral forms and ask your audience for referrals. In return you will give them a free report, audio download, or copy of your PowerPoint. This strategy works great if you are looking for specific business referrals.

For instance, one of my clients works with individuals with a net worth of over $5 million. You don't find such people in everyday audiences. To find them, he asks for referrals:

"Out of all the people you know, who do you know with a net worth of $5 million or more?"

The people in the audience may not have that kind of money but they may know a person who does.

Invite them to ask questions. You can invite your audience to ask you questions after the meeting as described in the Q and A section. This could be your entire invitation.

Sell from the stage. Offer one of your entry level programs, either a simple CD or DVD set or a more sophisticated program. This creates the ultimate action. People take out their credit cards and purchase your program. They become immediate clients and you make money.

In short, an invitation gives your audience the opportunity to take the next step with you, whatever that next step is.

In the next chapter I will teach you step-by-step how to execute each invitation like a pro and get your audience off their duff.

We have two more steps in our close.

4. Thank your audience

This is the time to express appreciation to your audience for their attention and participation. Thank them with, "You've been a great audience, I appreciate your time and energy!"

Don't use the word "Thank you" here. If you do, the audience won't give you a chance to finish your speech. They are trained to clap the minute you say thank you. Instead, use words such as "I appreciate...."

Now, the final step in the *close*.

5. Memorable statement

These are your final words to your audience. This is the statement, thought, or feeling you want to leave them with. Make it powerful. Make it memorable.

I end every speech with this memorable statement, "If you can't say it, you can't sell it!"

Here's a word of caution. Do not deliver your memorable statement and then say, "thank you." You have already thanked your audience. This memorable statement must be your final words.

13

Choose the Right Invitation for the Right Audience

The biggest mistake business speakers make is no call to action.
--Arvee Robinson

In the last chapter, I promised to teach you step-by-step how to use the five different Invitation strategies. This is one of the most important choices you will make because this is where you personalize the close for the needs of your audience. This is where you set yourself up to get the maximum results. For instance, if you are trying to sell a $5,000 program to a Kiwanis Club in twenty minutes, forget it! It won't work. Be sure to select the Invitation strategy that will best fit your topic, your audience, the length of time you are scheduled to speak and your personal level of speaking experience. This is the key to sales success from the platform.

Before using these strategies, you may need to get permission from the organizer or promoter of the event where you are speaking. For example, if you want to collect business cards, sign people up for a free coaching session or sell from the platform, get permission first. Most promoters forbid speakers to gather audience contact information because they worked hard getting the audience there and they don't want the speaker stealing their contacts. Many organizers don't allow speakers to sell from the stage because they promised their audience there would be no selling.

Whatever the reason, it is imperative that you ask the person who invited you to speak for permission. Ask this question before you develop your speech, not when you arrive at the scene. By then, it is too late.

Strategy #1: The business card strategy

At the beginning of your invitation, you raise your right hand and with great enthusiasm you shout, "How many of you like free stuff!"

Most people will raise their hand. If not, say, "By a show of hands."

To gather 100% of the business cards in the room, you must create desire. Show them what they are going to win, handle the product with respect, and tell them how much it is worth. You want to make your offer so irresistible your audience can't wait to participate.

Here's the script I use:

During this entire process, I hold the CD set so everyone can see the cover. "Great! I'm going to give one lucky person this three audio CD set called *How to Be a Networking Superstar*." I open the case and display each CD. I treat the entire package with respect. "The first CD has two formulas, one is how to create a killer elevator pitch and the second is how to turn it into a magnetic self-introduction. The second CD has a longer formula to create a 60-second self-introduction and a mini five-minute showcase. The third CD is full of networking tips such as how to work a room, how to break into small groups and three great escapes. The entire CD set sells on my website for $70. Today, one of you will take it home for free."

Next, I hold up a business card and say, "Everyone take out a business card!"

Pause until it's quiet.

Then I say, "You can participate in this raffle by placing your business card in this bag (hold up a 4x8x12 gift bag that reflects your brand). I would like to enter you into my database and send you weekly public speaking video tips and invitations to live events. If you want to be in the raffle but don't want to be in my database, fold the card in half. This will signal my assistant not enter you in my database. Sound good?"

Anyone who did not fold their card has given you permission to enter them in your database and market to them in the future.

Step three, invite a volunteer from the audience to help you collect the cards. Ask for your volunteer's name and then address the audience, "Pass your cards to the center aisle and *Mary* will pick them up."

Networking meetings will serve food, often at round tables with no clear center aisle. To make this process move fast, your volunteer needs to know where to go to collect the cards. In this case, say, "Pass your cards to the person with the longest hair."

Once I made the mistake of saying the opposite, "Pass your cards to the person with the *shortest* hair." I got a loud roar of laughter from the audience because there were bald men sitting at the tables. I don't know if I offended anyone. I play it safe now and use the *longest* hair.

Don't present essential information while your volunteer is collecting the cards, or it will get lost in the commotion. Say, "Quickly, quickly."

Once the business cards have been gathered and your volunteer returns with the bag (or whatever you are using to collect the cards), their instinct will be to give you the bag and sit down. Encourage them to stay and select the winner.

There are several reasons to ask your volunteer to pick a card.

1. **Audience participation.** Anytime you get the opportunity for a member of your audience to participate, take it. As human beings, we live through the experiences of others. By inviting a member of the audience to participate, you've created a way others can experience what they are doing. This will keep your listeners' attention.

2. **Eliminate the possibility of being biased.** As the speaker, you don't want to be responsible for picking one winner and having the rest for your audience mad at you.

3. **Struggle to read the card.** If you are over 40 years old, you may have trouble reading the tiny print often used on business cards. As the speaker, you don't want to fumble around with your reading glasses. So again, it is much easier for you to select a young person from your audience who doesn't need glasses or a person who is already wearing them.

4. **Mispronounce their name.** With today's diversity of cultures, it is common to have people with challenging last names. To eliminate the risk of mispronunciation and embarrassment, let the volunteer call the winner's name.

5. **Where are they?** Chances are your volunteer, if a member of the group, will know where that person is seated. They will let you know by looking in that direction.

Once the winner has been announced, take the card from the volunteer's hand and replace it with the gift. This will counteract the participant's instinct to give the winning business card back to its owner.

Now, you have a bag full of warm leads.

Strategy #2: Offer a free coaching, training or strategy session

I've been using this strategy for years. However, it didn't work well until I changed the language.

I used to invite prospects to a "free coaching" session at the end of my talk. I had the script down and close to 100% of the audience signed up. One problem. When my assistant called to schedule their appointment, they didn't return her call. The few that did get scheduled often didn't show up and those that did show up for the scheduled call expected a free 30-minute speech-coaching session.

I gave a lot of 30-minute coaching calls, but nobody bought.

The main reason to schedule time with a prospect is to learn more about what they do, their biggest challenge, and how you can help them. By the end of the call, you've determined how you can help them, recommended a program that fits their needs, and closed them for the business.

When a client expects a free coaching session, it sets the tone for a different conversation that doesn't support them or pay you for your time.

Then one day I heard a colleague invite her audience to a free strategy session.

At that moment I thought, "That's it - the word strategy is brilliant!"

Since then, I've changed my language from free coaching session to a free strategy session and it's made all the difference in the world.

I made a second change, empower those requesting a 30-minute strategy session to call me for their scheduled appointments instead of me calling them. Giving them this instruction reduced the number of no shows. It worked.

Of course, the occasional person doesn't show up, but these are far fewer than before. The best part of using the words "strategy session" is the prospects don't know what to expect so they arrive with an open mind. My close rate has tripled.

Before you schedule your first appointment, create a formal questionnaire that will help you find out more about your prospect's business and help you go from one question to the next. Use these same questions during every strategy session.

Next, develop your closing script. Know what products and services you are going to offer based on the answers to the questions. Invite your prospect to take the next step.

Here is the script I use to open the call and manage expectations:

"Are you ready for our call?"

"Yes." says the prospect.

"Great! Let me share with you how the call is going to go today. First, I'm going to ask you questions about your business. Next, I'll share ideas with you on how you can use public speaking to get more business. At the end of our call I'll recommend ways I can help you to do that, sound good?"

"Yes."

Use this persuasive technique. Begin asking questions about their business. Be sure to take notes. Write down your prospect's desires in their language so you can use it in your close.

Strategy #3: Ask for referrals

If you are selective about the type, size, skill, or financial level of your potential clients, the best way to generate quality leads is to ask for specific individuals or companies who meet your requirements.

The first step is to create a referral form. On the top of the form, capture the name and phone number of the individual giving you the referral.

Next, create a series of lines for the referral giver to write the names, phone numbers and email addresses of the businesses they are referring to you.

From the stage, announce that you are looking for referrals and will offer an item of value in exchange for the referrals.

Your script will sound like this:

"My business thrives on referrals. Out of all the people you know in the (blank) business, who do you know who would be a great referral for me?"

"For trusting me with your referrals, I will give you a copy of my free report on (blank) worth $97."

When you use this script, fill in the first (blank) with your industry and the second with the title of your free gift. Then assign an appropriate value to your gift. Collect the forms and you have dozens of quality referrals. Follow up on these leads within 24 hours and send the referral source a thank you note and the gift you promised them.

Strategy #4: Invite them to ask questions.

This strategy draws out the hot prospects in the room. Think of your audience as a haystack and you as the magnet drawing the needles out of the haystack. When you ask people to speak to you at the end of your talk, prospects who are interested in learning more about you will approach you.

Here is the script:

"I know you have a lot of questions, and I want to answer them. I'll be standing right here. Please feel free to come up to me at the end of my talk and ask any question you like."

As a speaker, you are viewed as a celebrity. Your audience needs permission to approach you.

Those who approach you after your talk are hot sizzling leads who may have a question, comment or want to buy your products or services. Expect several people to line up to speak to you. If you attempt to talk to everyone in line, they will lose interest and give up. And you will lose business.

Here's how I solve this problem. When a person approaches me at the end of my talk to ask a question, I respond, "That's a great question and I want to answer it. Would it be alright with you if I call you tomorrow?"

The prospect says, "Yes."

I then ask, "May I have your business card?"

They hand it to me. To identify them as a hot sizzling lead without breaking eye contact, I hold the card where they can't see it and bend the corner. The next day, as promised, I call them to schedule their 30-minute strategy session.

Strategy #5: Sell from the stage

This is the most challenging and the most lucrative invitation. To be successful you need to be trained, rehearsed, and have many hours of speaking experience.

Many powerful speakers use a specific formula to sell from the platform and make millions.

Before I share this money-making formula, let's talk about how much speaking time you have. If you have thirty minutes or less, you won't have enough time to sell at the end of your speech.

To create the best stage selling experience you need a minimum of 45 to 90 minutes to speak. When you have more time in front of your audience, they will resonate with your message, fall in love with you, and want to work with you. This will create the excitement that leads your audience to rush to the back of the room and buy more of your products, no matter how much the cost.

Your close will take five to fifteen minutes depending on the length of time of your speech lasts and the amount of the investment. The bigger the investment, the longer it takes to sell it.

If you hate selling, here's an idea that may change the way you think.

You hold the solution to your prospect's problem. You know that person is suffering, and you know they want a permanent solution that only you can provide. It is your moral duty to share your solutions, which can save their business or life. You can't accomplish this in a 30-minute presentation. You can only create awareness or a small breakthrough.

It took God seven days (including a day of rest) to create the world. How can we expect to create permanent change in others with one 90-minute speech? Change requires transformation, which happens over time through the high-end coaching and training programs you sell in your longer speech.

You must learn how to sell so you can help people and businesses achieve lasting change and success.

To do that, they need to sign up for one of your products or services. Don't think of it as selling, instead think of it as inviting them to take the next step with you and create amazing transformations that will change their businesses and lives forever.

The basic formula (which can be modified based on topic, audience, or product) for selling from the platform is:

- Name of the program
- Who is it for?
- What they will learn?
- Program location and date
- What is the investment?

- What are the bonuses?
- Limitation
- Special drop price
- Payment options
- Money back guarantee
- Tell them where to go to get it

The Invitation is the crucial step of your close. Select the right one for your audience, length of time you will speak, and your topic. No matter what, don't skip the Invitation.

Part III

The Prep:
How to Get Ready to
Deliver Your Powerful
Presentation

15

POP! Prepare and Over Practice

Practice until you become the speech.
--Arvee Robinson

If you want your presentation to POP, you must prepare your speech, your materials, and yourself ahead of time.

If it's a large group or a group that I am not familiar with, I prepare by visiting the organization the week or month before to find out how I can best serve them.

One time I fought through Los Angeles commuter traffic to attend the meeting of mediators the month before I spoke to chat with the members. During the conversation, I asked, "When it comes to public speaking, what is your biggest challenge?" They were more than happy to share their thoughts with me. This helped me customize my speech for them.

Using this valuable information, I customized my signature talk to fit this group by adding their language and examples and titled it, *How to Use Public Speaking to Grow Your Mediation Business.* I was a big hit! I gathered over 50 warm leads and sold

$7,000 worth of speaker training, all because I cared enough to invest extra time getting to know what the group wanted.

Imagine you have a speaking engagement. Now what?!

This step-by-step guide will prepare you for speaking success. Every step is important. If you leave one out, it could cost you leads, sales, and future speaking engagements.

1. Find out as much as you can.

When a meeting organizer invites you to speak to their organization, ask them where the venue is, how many people will be in the audience, what time you will speak, and for how long. It is important to find out as much as you can about your audience and what they want. If you can't attend a meeting, you can gather information from the Internet and by talking to the organizer. Always ask for the cell number of the main contact person. This has often saved me from getting lost while driving to the event.

2. Create a speaking folder.

Organize your speaking engagements by creating a folder for each one. In this folder, file the above checklist and all other essential information such as handouts, flyers, and emails. I use purple folders to identify them. Label the top with the date and name of the speaking engagement, for example: 09-12-12 NAWP (National Association of Women Professionals). File it in a hanging folder labeled "Upcoming Speaking Engagements." Take this folder with you when you speak.

Here's how it can save the day. One morning I was driving to a speaking engagement in an unfamiliar city. I followed the MapQuest all the way to the right street, but the address didn't exist. I drove up and down the street but no luck. I pulled over to the curb, and called my contact's cell number. He didn't answer. I picked up my speaker folder and found a flyer about the event. At the bottom of the flyer, I found the host's name and number. To my surprise, he answered and guided me to the right location. It turned out that the street was divided into East and West sections. I was on the wrong one. Thank goodness for the flyer in my speaker folder.

3. Customize your speech.

Now that you have researched the group, customize your speech with what you've learned. Don't develop a new speech. Instead, modify twenty percent of your standard signature talk. Use their industry lingo, stories, and testimonials in your revised speech. The more you talk like your audience, the more they will love you, trust you, and buy from you.

4. Practice, practice, practice.

Once you've customized your speech for your new audience, it is time to practice. Rehearse one hour for every two minutes of your speech. For instance, if you are preparing a 30-minute presentation, practice a minimum of 15 hours.

Several years ago, Adam Urbanski, one of my mentors, asked me to speak on his stage. Adam invited several speakers to present and gave us each 15 minutes.

When my turn to speak arrived, Adam asked if I needed a timer. I replied no. After my speech, Adam said, "You nailed it, right to the minute! I should have known. You're a pro."

I nailed it because I practiced my speech over and over again. Even after speaking for over 30 years, I still rehearse one hour for every two minutes I speak.

When you practice your speech, speak it aloud. You will achieve far greater results faster by speaking and hearing it than you would if you roll it around in your head forever. If you are tempted to write your speech out word for word, never read it or you will become a prisoner of your own words. By outlining your speech as we discussed in Chapter 10 and hearing it aloud, you can make appropriate adjustments on the spot. You may even add a story or an exercise. This gives you the freedom to modify your presentation as you go and to speak from the heart.

5. Develop your PowerPoint Presentation.

Since the advent of PowerPoint, many speakers are confused as to whether they should create a PowerPoint presentation for their speech. If in doubt, don't. In case you are still thinking about it, here is the rule of thumb I use:

Use PowerPoint only under these circumstances:

a) You are speaking for 90 minutes or more and you are selling from the platform.

b) You are in your own room where you can control the environment.

c) You are playing an important video or showing before and after pictures.

That's it.

There are many reasons not to use PowerPoint. First, speakers often use it as a crutch. Second, it is easy for the speaker to read from and speak to the screen instead of to their audience. Third, your audience will tend to look at your PowerPoint instead of at you. You are the presentation, not your PowerPoint.

When speakers see other speakers use PowerPoint, they often feel like they need to use it too, which is not always the case.

This happened to me.

At Adam Urbanski's event, the other 15-minute speakers all used PowerPoint presentations. For a moment, I thought to myself, "Hmmm, maybe I should put a PowerPoint together." The stage stood five feet above the audience and stretched across the room. On the right of the stage a huge screen towered over the speaker. I watched each speaker turn to look at their PowerPoint, exposing their backside to the audience every time the slide changed. Who wants to connect with the speaker's backside? Nobody! When you talk to the screen and not to the audience, you disconnect from the people you most want to hear your message.

I dismissed the idea and created an interactive experience with my audience.

The less time you speak, the more you need to stay connected to your audience. You connect with them every time you look and speak to them. This connection will get your audience to fall in love with you, lead them to desire more, and later buy.

6. Print your speaker introduction.

In chapter 12, I gave you the template for creating a powerful speaker introduction. Before you print your introduction, customize it to fit your audience and your talk. After you print it, file it in your speaker folder and take it with you. I print my speaker introduction using 22-point type, so my introducer can read it with ease.

7. Prepare yourself ahead of time.

This includes what you plan to wear and how you show up. Well before the event, decide the appropriate attire for the group and make sure that it is clean, pressed and ready to go. Get your hair cut or styled days before your speaking engagement. The night before, get plenty of sleep to keep your energy high. Don't forget to gas up and wash your car. You communicate volumes when you show up in a dirty car.

One time after I finished speaking at a women's group in Arizona, one of the members offered to drive me to the airport.

When I stepped into her car, my feet landed on a messy pile of empty cups and fast food wrappers. Her specialty was marketing. Although she may have been good at it, her car told me she was unorganized and didn't take pride in herself. As a result, I would never hire her, even to this day.

8. Prepare your speaker bag.

You may be asking yourself, "What is a speaker bag?" It is a carrying case for all your speaking information and products. Include in this bag your handouts, directions, product giveaways, empty bag for your raffle, speaker introduction, offer forms and credit card forms (if you are selling a product), camera, your speaker folder, and whatever else you need to take with you. This bag can also serve as a reminder that you have an upcoming speaking event.

I save Mondays for special projects. One Monday I sat down at my desk ready to start my day, and glanced at my conference table. To my horror, I saw my speaker bag ready to go. I had forgotten that I was speaking that morning! I jumped up, changed my clothes, and ran out the door. Lucky for me the speaking engagement was fifteen minutes away. I arrived on time and delivered an inspirational presentation to a group of unemployed individuals. After my talk, several of them shared that my speech gave them hope. If I hadn't noticed my speaker bag on the table, I would have missed that opportunity.

9. Plan to arrive 30 minutes early.

This one step will eliminate potential stress and keep you calm before your presentation. It will also give you extra time for unexpected traffic or other events. It is important to arrive before most of the attendees to prepare your speaking environment. On arrival, find out where you are going to speak, set up your speaking area, and select where you will sit before and after your talk.

Where you sit is important. Since most networking groups are scheduled around a meal, either breakfast, lunch or dinner, the room will be set up with round tables that sit six to eight people.

Arriving early allows you to select your seat, unless the organizer has selected one for you (which is seldom the case). Select the center-front table and sit in the seat closest to the speaking area. Prepare your notes, handouts, and raffle prize there before you speak.

Once you have your seat and you've set your stage, find the person who is going to introduce you and give them your speaker introduction. Ask them to read it out loud in front of you. This will familiarize them with it and make sure they pronounce your name right. Then ask your introducer if they plan to stay on stage until you arrive and shake your hand, or will they walk off stage. If they say they are going to walk off stage, this could create an awkward moment. A tip I learned from the Toastmaster International program is to "*never leave the stage unattended.*" Encourage your introducer to stay on stage until you arrive to greet them. Think of it like passing the baton. You want to create a professional transition from introducer to speaker.

When you arrive at your speaking engagement early, you can greet other guests as they arrive and begin to build trust, rapport, and friendships with your audience. The more trust and rapport you build, the more money you make.

10. Plan to eat with your audience.

Most networking groups, conferences, and seminars center their meetings around a meal. Don't miss this opportunity to meet and talk with your audience. Celebrity speakers often wait in the hall or in another room, called the "green room" until they speak. Others are afraid to eat before they speak. Both are a big mistake. These speakers alienate themselves from their audience before they even start talking. Instead, use this time to get acquainted with your future prospects and clients. Ask questions and get to know them to build trust and rapport before you speak. This personal connection will increase your results at the end of your talk.

11. Make the final preparations.

After you eat with the audience and before dessert is served, make last-minute preparations for your talk. Prepare your handouts ahead of time to distribute to the audience, ask a volunteer to help you when it's time, and set the final stage with your products and forms.

16

Use Notes Without Distraction

Keep your listeners, not your notes, in the palm of your hand.
--Arvee Robinson

Years ago, I delivered my second Toastmasters speech, five to seven minutes on "Speak with Sincerity." I was shocked when I read the words "try it without notes." This was a new concept. To me, notes range from a short outline to a full written speech. In corporate America, I always wrote out my speech and used the complete script when I spoke.

When I gave the Toastmaster speech, I discovered you don't need to use notes in short speeches. However, when I gave 60-90 minute business presentations, I realized I still needed notes to keep my speech on track but I didn't want to go back to the old model of writing out my speech. Without notes, I connected with my audience at a deeper level, and built rapport faster. I wanted notes and deeper connections. So here is my solution. I create an outline and turn it into a one-page audience handout and use that during my speech as my notes. It works like a charm.

The three most acceptable types of notes are 1) an outline 2) audience handout, and 3) PowerPoint slides. Do not use a full-blown, hand-written speech as your notes. Writing out your entire speech will tempt you to read it or memorize it. Either way, you become a prisoner of your words and don't connect with your audience. You make the same mistake I made when speaking to an audience of 300 people in corporate America, lose your place, get frustrated, and run off the stage.

Or it could be even worse. I remember attending a multi-speaker convention in a huge sports arena. There must have been 10,000 people surrounding the stage. Most of the speakers were excellent. Then there was a pause. The organizers moved an acrylic lectern onto the stage. The emcee introduced a relative of a famous business icon. She walked on stage with a pile of papers in her hand, plopped them down onto the lectern, and began to read. The effect was immediate. The energy level in the room collapsed as she droned on. A potentially powerful speech went flat and her rapport with the audience vanished. She will forever stand out as the one boring speaker in a long list of motivational stars.

For longer speeches without PowerPoint, you can use an outline without distracting your audience. Many high-paid motivational speakers use this method for their longer presentations.

When I was in corporate America working as a systems consultant, I often attended huge software conventions. At one of them, I arrived early and sat in the front row. There were 3,000 people in the audience. The keynote speaker was motivating, entertaining, and captivating.

Half way through his talk he walked over to the lectern, picked up his water glass and took a drink.

Because I sat in the front row, I saw him glance down at his speech outline, take a sip, return the glass to its original position and continue to talk, all without distracting his audience. Brilliant move.

On another occasion, the opposite effect happened. I watched in horror as a famous keynote speaker waved her notes around for 90-minutes. She would stop, flip through them, read one of them, then turn back to the audience and continue her speech. HUGE distraction. It cost her clients, sales, and reputation.

Follow these guidelines. If your speech is under 15 minutes, don't use notes. Your speech is short enough that with the appropriate amount of practice you will know the script well enough to deliver it with ease. For a 30- to 45-minute speech, create an outline then turn it into a handout for your audience to follow. Use this handout as your notes. For a speech over 60 minutes, use either an outline or create a PowerPoint presentation.

17

Create a Handout People Want to Keep

Add your picture and contact information on every handout.
--Arvee Robinson

Handouts are used for four specific reasons, for speeches fifteen to forty-five minutes long, and when you are not selling from the stage.

The four reasons are:

1. **To enhance the learning experience.** The three primary learning modalities are, audio, visual and kinesthetic. Audio learners learn best by listening to your presentation and may or may not take notes. Your visual learners will appreciate colorful pictures on your handout or PowerPoint presentation. The kinesthetic learners love to experience what you are talking about and will be the first to participate in your presentation.

They take copious notes and keep your handout for later review.

2. **They have your contact information.** Your handout is a tactful way to give your audience your contact information so they can contact you later. Make sure it includes your phone number, email address, and website at the bottom of your handout.

3. **They remember you.** Add your picture and a brief biography to your handout so your audience will remember you. Use a color headshot that looks like you and is no more than two years old. Place it to the left of your bio. In your bio, describe what you do for your clients and customers in 75 words or less. Set your type size smaller than the rest of your handout so it doesn't dominate the page.

4. **They can follow along.** Your handout guides your audience through your speech. From the beginning they know what you are going to talk about, how much material you're going to cover, and when you will finish your talk.

Before one of my talks to a real estate group, I decided to test this handout theory so I didn't create a handout. When I ended my speech, a lady in the front row screamed at the top of her lungs, "Is that all there is?!" She was so absorbed in my presentation that she didn't see the end coming. I realized at that moment how important a handout is. I seldom give a speech without one unless I'm selling from the stage and using PowerPoint.

Follow these basic guidelines when you create handouts for your audience:

1. **Use one sheet of paper.** You can use one or both sides for your handout. Do not use multiple pieces of paper.

Every time an audience member turns a page, the noise will distract them from hearing your speech.

2. **Make it interesting and fun.** Add color and design to your handout. Keep it professional because it represents you as a speaker. Make your handout pleasing to the eye so your audience will want to write on it and keep it.

3. **Create an easy learning experience.** Studies show that when people take notes they retain more of what they learned at a deeper level. The best way to encourage this is to use fill-in-the-blank segments in your handout.

4. **Add the meat.** The information on your handout includes the meat of your presentation. Do not include the opening or closing portion of your speech.

Your handout design can take many different forms as long as it looks professional. You can use fill-in-the-blank with one word answers or entire sentences, fill-in circles on a page, or other images. Be creative, make it easy to follow, and attractive to keep.

There are two situations when you do NOT need to use a handout, when you are speaking for one hour or more and selling an expensive program at the end of your talk and when your talk is 15 minutes or less.

In the first case, if you give them a handout when you are selling from the stage they will go home with a piece of you and don't have to buy your program.

In the second case, when you have 15 minutes or less to speak, you need every minute of that to build rapport with your audience and get them to fall in love with you. When you pass out a handout you'll use five minutes to distribute it, the audience will spend the next five minutes reading it, and by the time they look up to hear what you're saying you'll only have five minutes left.

Have you ever noticed stage-selling speakers never have business cards? It's for the same reason. If an audience member can take home a business card, they can put off a buying decision. Be careful what you hand out. It could cost you the sale.

See Appendix 6 for several examples of handouts I use.

18

Powerful PowerPoint Pointers

Remember, you, not your PowerPoint, are the presentation.
--Arvee Robinson

For years, I rebelled against using PowerPoint for my speeches. Back when I was working in corporate America, I endured the first PowerPoint presentations ever given. Most of them were dull and boring, and even worse, the projectors were so bad you had to turn out the lights to see the slides. What happens when you watch a boring presentation in the dark? You fall asleep! You can't persuade or influence your audience if they doze off. Your job as a presenter is to captivate your audience, not put them to sleep.

Years later, when I started my public speaking training company and began to speak and sell from big stages, I realized that PowerPoint is no longer the dull, bullet-driven, audience snoozer it used to be. PowerPoint, enhanced with pictures and video, can be your best friend when giving longer speeches, one hour or more, and/or selling from the stage, if you use it right.

103

PowerPoint is a tool, NOT the presentation – YOU are the presentation.

For example, my friend and book coach Lee Pound tells a story about his photographer dad and a Brahma bull. Through most of the story the PowerPoint screen is blank. At the critical moment, when he describes his dad taking the most dramatic photo of his career, Lee clicks to the next PowerPoint slide, which shows that exact photo. The effect is electric.

You can also use PowerPoint to keep you on track. The tricky part is that you have to know which slide is next. Otherwise, a slide you are not expecting may surprise you. If this happens your audience will notice jerkiness in your delivery, which will break the connection with them.

When you develop your slide presentation use the following guidelines.

Minimize bullet points. Instead use photographs along with text to give it a visual dimension, make stories come alive, and add emotion.

Make your text BIG. Start with 36-point fonts for titles and 26-point fonts for supporting information. The larger the better.

Avoid complete sentences, which are dull and hard to read. Large amounts of text will cause your audience to disconnect from you. The only exceptions are quotes and testimonials used to create a specific emotional impact.

Instead of fancy scrolled or script fonts, use easy-to-read fonts like Verdana, Helvetica, or Arial.

When presenting, don't turn away from your audience to look at your PowerPoint screen. This disconnects you from your audience and could cost you thousands of dollars in sales. Instead, position your laptop computer or monitor in front of you so you can see your presentation without looking away from your audience. If this isn't possible, turn your head, not your entire body, toward the screen.

When using PowerPoint, never turn out the lights. Years ago, projectors were not as powerful as today's technology and required dimming the lights. With modern PowerPoint equipment, this isn't necessary.

19

Look the Part

Don't let your clothes speak louder than you.
--Arvee Robinson

Students often ask me, "What do I wear when I speak?" When selecting the right wardrobe, think about your audience, topic, venue, and yourself. You will find as many do's as don'ts. Let's talk about the do's first.

Audience. Dress with your audience in mind. Are they business professionals or stay-at-home moms? Show them respect and dress one step up from the way they dress.

Topic. Your audience will expect you to dress in a certain way based on your topic. If you are a fitness coach, your audience will expect a nice workout outfit instead of a stuffy business suit. If your speech is about creating sales, look like a successful salesperson.

Venue. Location plays an important role in what you wear when you speak. A few years ago I presented my one-day Persuasive Speaking Mastery workshop in Hawaii.

My client Janet, who lives there, called me on the phone and said, "You're not going to wear your dark navy blue suit are you?"

"Yes, I am," I replied.

"It's casual here, Arvee. Wear bright clothes!"

That was good information. I selected a casual, bright red suit that fit my audience and location better. Be sure to ask questions about the venue and bring two or three outfits in case you need to make a quick change.

Yourself. Because I came out of the Corporate world, wearing a business suit when I speak is comfortable and authentic for me. However, it's not for everyone. Dress in a way that is authentic for you, your image and your brand.

Matt Bacak, a multi-millionaire, stepped on our stage wearing tan shorts and a black silk short-sleeve shirt. Over dinner, he confessed to my business partner Lee Pound and I that he had a suit and tie in his suitcase. "You didn't mention the shorts when we talked earlier so I didn't change," he added. It worked for him because he is a casual guy who makes a lot of money.

Clothing can also become your brand. My client Marlon Call is known as the insurance cowboy. When he speaks, he dresses in a nice pair of jeans, chaps, a long-sleeved shirt with his logo embroidered on the back, and wears a clean cowboy hat. He greets his audience with a loud yee-hah!

Eliminate distractions. After you've selected your speaking outfit, eliminate any item that may distract the audience from listening to your talk.

For example: Women, avoid dangle earrings, gaudy jewelry, open toe shoes, hair in the face, eye glasses, psychedelic patterns or stripes, polka dots, animal prints, and low-cut tops. Men, avoid loud ties, pocket protectors filled with pens, and cell phone holsters.

Don't wear name badges. Early in my speaking career I was asked to speak at a networking group. I was super excited. When I walked into the meeting room, the gal at the door gave me a sticky name badge. I peeled off the back, placed it on my right shoulder, and forgot about it. When my turn to speak came, I noticed my badge was gone. Without a second thought, I delivered my 30-minute presentation. When I returned to my seat, I looked down, and to my horror, my name badge was stuck upside down on my belly! It's best to never put on a name badge of any kind because you never know where it will end up.

Bottom line: When giving a presentation, dress your dressiest, authentic self, congruent with your audience, topic, and venue. Eliminate all distractions that prevent your audience from focusing on you and your message.

Part IV

The Delivery:
Bring Your Presentation to
Life!

20

Speak from the Heart

The best speeches come from the heart.
-Arvee Robinson

People say, "I speak from the heart."

What does that mean?

Novice presenters believe it means they don't need to prepare. To them, speaking from the heart means jumping on the stage with no plan or training, mouthing a few stale clichés, saying thank you, and walking off to thunderous silence.

They are wrong! Speaking from the heart happens after years of practice, preparation, and training. It is not a learned skill, it is a higher level of speaking. It appears when you are able to reach deep into your innermost self, connect to your message, and know how it impacts your audience.

One day, I was speaking to a group of over a hundred people. All of a sudden, I entered *"the zone."* The closest way to describe it is total focus on the message without thinking about it. In the zone, the most amazing heartfelt message rose up out of my soul, rolled off my lips, and floated into the audience. "Each and every one of you has a message to share that only you can share to people that can only hear it from you!"

A man in the front row said, "Wow, that is profound!"

In that moment, I got it. *Speaking from the heart* is more than speaking with passion. It's connecting your heart with your audience's heart. When you are in the zone, you sense the exact message your audience needs to hear. Brilliant words flow out of your mouth, touch them on a deep emotional level, and change their lives. You say to yourself, "That was great! Where did those words come from?"

When you reach this higher level of speaking, you will know it, and your audience will sense it and experience breakthroughs and transformations.

It's rare for even experienced speakers to speak from their hearts for their entire speech. Most speakers go in and out of the zone. Most beginning speakers never reach the zone. It takes years of practice, commitment, and dedication to reach the heart connection.

To reach this level, you need to be yourself, focus on your audience, speak with passion, and above all practice.

Be Yourself. When speaking from the heart you must be authentic. Many novice speakers think they have to act like other speakers they have seen on stage. This is not true. You must bring your own unique gifts and style to your presentations. There is one you. If you pretend to be anyone else, your audience will know it. Be real with yourself, your message and your audience.

Think about your audience. Speak every word with your audience in mind. Focus on what they want and give it to them in the way they want to hear it. Use their language and use stories and references from their world. If you are speaking to realtors, use real estate lingo to give them the experience they expect.

Speak with passion. Passion comes from the heart. When you speak with passion your audience will feel it. Your voice is filled with enthusiasm, excitement and energy. This passion captivates your audience and keeps them on the edge of their seats. Passion sells.

To speak with passion you must be connected with your message and above all be passionate about it. Sounds logical, right? However, not every speaker is passionate about what they say or sell.

In one of my four-day speaker trainings, one of my students had this problem. His speech was dry, drab, and boring. He developed his signature talk to sell a popular energy drink and grow his network marketing team. During his speech, he described how one can gives you the energy of a five-year-old.

I thought to myself, "Maybe he should drink a can before he speaks."

When he finished talking, I asked him questions about the company he represented. It turns out this was not his passion! He shared that his true dream was to speak to audiences of teens and teach them how they can become teenage entrepreneurs. When he spoke about what he would teach, his eyes lit up, his energy picked up and he had a big smile on his face. He spoke with passion.

"That's it!" I screamed. "That's what you need to talk about!"

If you can't bring passion to a topic, you need to change topics. It's that simple. Speak what you are passionate about and the words will flow from your heart.

Practice. You can't speak from the heart without practice. You need to craft and rehearse your presentation. The more prepared you are the easier it will be to speak your words from your heart.

We've all heard the saying, "Practice makes perfect!"

Practice until you become the script. This will put you in "the zone," where you can speak from beyond the heart.

How do you grow from a heart connection to a soul connection?

You care more about the people in your audience than you do yourself. You possess an inner desire to help them and believe in your heart that your message will save their business or save their life!

21

Keep Them on the Edge
of Their Seats

Speakers must create an unforgettable audience experience.
--Arvee Robinson

Once you've conquered speaking from the heart and have learned how to grab your audience's attention at the beginning, the next challenge is to keep their attention for the rest of your presentation.

Today's audiences want more than to sit and listen. They want an experience. They want to participate in your presentation and have fun. They want rich content, presented in an entertaining fashion. Boring is out, it's so 1970s.

Back then, we paid to be lectured by professors, doctors, political figures, and celebrities and expected to be bored. And we were.

In the 1980s, speakers tried two different kinds of flash and sizzle to engage their audiences. One group become over-the-top actors, and the second group, techno-geeks, used bright colors and fancy graphics on PowerPoint screens in darkened rooms. All they accomplished was to convert boring lectures into inauthentic performances.

By the end of the decade, it became clear that neither approach worked. Replacing the old overhead projectors and their dull black and white slides with the new glamorous PowerPoint didn't make presentations more interesting, it made them worse.

When the speakers disappeared into PowerPoint darkness, they disconnected from their audience, the slides became the presentation, and the audience went to sleep.

On the other hand, the actors kept their audiences awake with a 'rah, rah' performance but gave little substance. The audience went home exhausted, wondering why they attended in the first place. Presentations still bored people, in a different manner.

By the 1990's, audiences, tired of dark rooms and over-the-top presenters, demanded more connection with speakers. They wanted to feel like they were having a conversation with the presenter in their living room. Speakers responded by being more authentic and encouraging greater audience participation.

Today, audiences expect the speaker to create an emotional experience that connects them with the speaker and with each other. They have fun, learn by experience, and become part of the presentation.

You do this by involving them in your speech, which will captivate your listeners, enhance your speaking ability, and elevate your sales.

Here are a few examples of the many ways you can involve your audience and create an exciting, emotional, and memorable experience.

Let's play with words

A great way to get your audience to participate (and my personal favorite) is by commanding them to repeat what you say.

For example, my signature phrase is: "How cool is that?! Say that's cool." My audience will say "That's cool."

Another way is to ask them a direct question, "There are seven ways to become a persuasive speaker. How many ways?" They answer, "Seven."

Another idea is to encourage them to finish your sentence without you telling them what to say.

For example you could use a popular phrase, "People buy from people they know, like and . . . (pause)," the audience finishes the sentence with "TRUST."

My personal favorite is when I talk about how powerful our words are. "God said, let there be light, and there was .. (pause)," the audience replies, "Light!" He made us in his own (pause), the audience replies, "Image!"

This idea works best if the sentence is a popular phase your audience has heard before. Make sure that it is a sentence they know how to finish.

I made this mistake.

When I was speaking at Chris Howard's Billionaire Adventure Club on a cruise down the Nile River, I used a commercial popular in the United States in the 1950's, "When EF Hutton speaks..." I didn't realize that only two people in this international audience came from the U.S. and the rest were from other countries. They all stared back at me with puzzled expressions. I realized my mistake. My audience had never heard this commercial and had no idea how to respond. I delivered the punch line, "everybody listens," and moved on. I learned a big lesson. Make every example fit your audience.

Let's get physical!

Audience participation doesn't have to be limited to repeating words or phrases. You can get physical and use their bodies to interact with each other. This is a powerful technique that can wake them up and change their mental state.

During my presentations, I ask for two volunteers from the audience to join me on stage to demonstrate how they can each use powerful body language to look and feel more confident.

This creates two kinds of involvement. The volunteers feel special and the audience participates through them.

In this example, I first ask the volunteers to introduce themselves. Then I demonstrate the proper speaker stance. I say, "Put your feet together." Then I show them how to do it.

When they are in the proper position, I ask, "Is it okay if I touch you?" When you get permission to touch a stranger you show them respect. Then touch them in the safe zone, on the arm between the elbow and shoulder.

Next, I give them a firm push to demonstrate how unstable this stance is.

Next I say, "Stand with your feet shoulder length apart. Imagine roots growing from the bottom of your feet. Put your chest out and your head back."

When they switch to this position, I give them another firm shove. This time they are solid as a rock.

Next, I invite the entire audience to pick a partner and experience the exercise for themselves. This locks the lesson in at a deep level.

You can also use more rigorous physical activities such as singing, clapping, or dancing.

Combine both physical and verbal techniques.

For example, in every speech, when I reach step 3 in my speaker system I say, "Raise your right hand, pat yourself on the back, and say, 'Good job for being here.' Now turn to the person next to you, pat their back, and say, 'Good job for being here.'"

As part of my attention grabber, I ask my audience, "How are you today?" Then I ask them to touch their hearts and say, "I'm blessed."

You can combine any physical act with any words or phrases that are appropriate to your speech and your audience. For instance, I've seen speakers ask their audience to turn to the person next to them, give them a high five, and say "This is great stuff!" Whatever you do, be careful not to overuse it.

Let's partner

In longer speeches, you can break the audience into small groups of two, three, or four and have them do an exercise. This creates instant rapport between your audience members. When using this technique, give your audience clear and concise instructions on what you want them to do, including the timeline and the expected outcome.

Partners of two are the easiest to control and take the least amount of time. These instructions for groups of two can be modified for use with larger groups.

1. Explain the exercise:

"In a moment, you will pick a partner. You will each have three minutes to share. When I say go, you will share with your partner (insert a subject related to the topic of your speech). When I call time, switch partners. Any questions?"

2. Pick a partner:

"Pick a partner you don't know (this allows people to meet a new person)."

3. Choose who goes first:

"Choose an A and a B, A goes first, GO!"

4. Time and switch:

"Three minutes are up, switch partners and GO!"

5. Complete the exercise:

"Time is up. Thank your partner for sharing."

6. Share the experience:

"Who would like to share?"

Invite as many people to participate as time permits. After each person shares, thank them.

You can use these and other creative ways to involve your listeners. Select the techniques that work best for you, your audience, and your topic.

22

Communicate with Your Entire Body

Make sure your body language is congruent with your message.
--Arvee Robinson

Body language speaks louder than we do.

Slight changes in your expressions or movements can cost you audience rapport, clients, and sales.

When you are the speaker, you must know what you are communicating, both verbal and non-verbal. Your gestures, expressions, and words work together to create a powerful, persuasive presentation. If any one of them is missing, your speech will bore your audience to tears.

It is also important that your gestures, expressions, and body movement are congruent with your words. Nothing turns an audience off faster than actions not matching words

First let's look at the most important body communicator, the eyes.

The eyes don't lie.

Have you ever talked to a person who doesn't look you in the eye? What are they saying? When a person looks away, it reveals dishonesty or a lack of confidence.

This applies to speakers too. When you speak, you must make eye contact with as many people in your audience as possible. If you don't, it will destroy confidence, credibility, and trust.

In smaller audiences of thirty or less you can maintain intimate eye contact with each member of the audience. Take about three to four seconds to look into the eyes of each person, then move on to the next. If you take any longer than that, the audience member will think you are staring, feel uncomfortable, turn away, and never look at you again.

When you move from person to person, make it smooth. Do not dart in and out or fly from one side of the room to the other. Make sure you make a connection before you move on.

In large audiences, it isn't possible to make eye contact with every individual. Instead, break your audience into four quadrants and spend time in each. Every person will think you are looking at them.

Before you start your speech, sweep the audience with your eyes. This will connect you with your audience and build rapport.

Consistent eye contact throughout your presentation conveys honesty, confidence, and trust. When you hold a person's eye, you hold their attention.

Hands are for gesturing.

Many of my students ask, "What do I do with my hands?"

"Don't worry about them," I replied, "as they are not a distraction."

Hand gestures add depth to your words. When you move your hands, these gestures must be congruent with what you say. They are like adjectives, they add an emotional element, add meaning to your words, and give your audience a visual experience.

For example, if you talk about the world being round, demonstrate by drawing a circle in the air. If you describe a person who is a square, draw a square using both hands together. If you tell a story about your five-year-old daughter, hold your hand out and down to show her height.

Use fun gestures. Hold your hand to your ear with your pinkie and thumb out to emulate a telephone or pretend to bounce a ball with an up-and-down hand motion.

Use your imagination. Be creative, plan every move, and practice.

Whatever gestures you choose to use, make them sharp, clean, and emphatic. Be committed to every gesture.

Not all gestures are created equal. Avoid inappropriate hand gestures like these:

- Pointing your finger at your audience. This will make them feel uncomfortable, as if you are scolding them. Instead, use an open palm when gesturing to your audience.
- Pounding your fist on a lectern or on your open palm. This aggressive gesture will make your listeners feel as though you are pounding them on the head.
- Using the same gesture too many times. This drives your audience crazy. They will start counting your gestures rather than listening to your message.
- Inappropriate gestures, including gestures that don't cross cultural boundaries. Do your homework to avoid making these mistakes.

Allow your hands to make natural movements, on purpose, as you practiced them. When you are not gesturing, hold your hands by your side.

Stand with power and confidence.

Have you ever seen a speaker lean on one hip or sway from side to side when they talked?

One of my students waltzed during his speech. He took one step back, stepped to the side, stepped forward, and stepped to the side again. He wasn't aware of this until I put a seven-inch gavel between his ankles and told him not to let it drop. Movement of this kind during your speech creates a BIG distraction for your audience. Distracted listeners lose interest, check out, and don't buy.

The way you stand on stage is silent communication that can destroy or enhance your connection with your audience. Many speakers lean on one hip, cross their legs, or sway back and forth, all of which steal your confidence, credibility, and power.

Stand in the rooted position, with your feet shoulder length apart, chest out, and chin up. Imagine roots growing from the bottom of your feet deep into the ground.

If you find yourself standing in the wrong position while speaking, adjust and get into the rooted position. You will look more confident and powerful as you speak.

Move with purpose

Pacing on stage is a huge distracter for audiences. When a speaker paces back and forth while they speak, it is difficult for the listeners to focus on what the speaker is saying and they often lose interest. It is better to stand in one spot and deliver your entire speech than to pace.

When you need to add movement, do it with purpose. Think before you move. If you want, move closer to an audience member, think about it, and then step into that position. If you want to look at your notes on the lectern, think about it and then walk there. Your audience can see your thoughts and understand your movement.

One of my first keynotes was for a group of trade school graduates. When I practiced my speech, I pictured the students sitting in front of me as I spoke from the stage. Their faces glowed with big smiles and wide eyes as they listened. I rehearsed each move and each gesture. I looked forward to delivering a performance that would inspire these young adults as they entered the work force.

I was not prepared for what I saw.

When I arrived empty chairs were lined up in perfect rows on the stage. "Why are there so many chairs on the stage?" I asked one of the instructors. He replied, "They're for the graduating students."

In five words, he destroyed my entire presentation plan. I'm going to have my backside to the most important part of my audience, the students. "What on earth do I do now?" I thought.

In the few minutes left, I looked at the audience section and turned and looked at the student session behind me. "Aha," I thought, "The chairs are in two sections with an aisle in the middle." I decided to stand in the aisle and gesture to the students behind me. I was careful not to walk in front of them or upstage them. The aisle was narrow so I stood still and let my hands do the moving.

Whether you choose to move or stand still, always do it with conviction and purpose.

23

Sweet Sounds
Made from Your Voice

Vary your pitch, tonality, and volume throughout your speech.
--Arvee Robinson

Your voice is your most powerful instrument. When you use it right, you will mesmerize your audience. When you use it wrong, you will bore them.

After you develop your speech, practice delivering it with the right volume, pitch, and rate. Let's take a look at each.

Volume. Vary your volume to keep your audience's attention. Use volume to emphasize a point or an emotion. For example, when you convey excitement or anger use louder volume. When you share a secret or sad story use softer volume.

Pitch. Don't drone on in a monotone voice that lulls your audience to sleep. Vary your pitch to keep them listening. When you're excited, use a higher pitch. When you are sad, use a lower pitch. At all times, make your pitch congruent with your message.

Rate. Your rate is the number of words you speak per minute. At times fast is appropriate and at times it's not.

Speak faster when you want to excite the audience, create a sense of urgency and emotion, increase tension, and show joy or happiness.

Speak slower when you want to let your audience catch their breath, tell a sad story, create a powerful emotional moment, or answer questions.

Power of the pause. Use after you emphasize an important point or story, pause to allow your audience time to digest what you've said.

If you forget what you were going to say, pause to collect your thoughts. Do not fill the silence with umhs or ahhhs. Be silent until you recover.

If your audience becomes distracted, use the pause to regain their attention. This will also silence any side conversations taking place during your speech.

Don't take your voice for granted. Before every speech, practice volume, pitch, rate, and pauses to create a powerful experience for your audience.

Part V

Before you Step on Stage:
It's a Scary New World Out
There. Prepare Yourself for
the Worst

24

Step into Your Discomfort Zone

When a speaking opportunity arises, say yes and then get ready.
--Arvee Robinson

Now you know how to craft your signature speech, stand with power, use your voice, and gesture with your hands. It's time to go beyond these basic skills, get moving, and stretch yourself. It's time to step into your discomfort zone.

Several years ago, I was an enrichment speaker on an 11-day Mediterranean cruise. My mentor threw me out of my comfort zone when he said, "You can't speak about public speaking. You have to come up with four new topics."

My head spun. No public speaking? "What on earth do I talk about?" I asked.

He said, "Look at the best sellers on Amazon and find a couple you resonate with."

The light bulb went on. I speak about communication. In a few minutes on Amazon, I picked the top two books on the subject, which took care of the first two topics I needed. With that success under my belt, I pulled two more new topics from my own experience. With four new speeches on topics I had never presented before, I jumped into my discomfort zone.

When Opportunity Knocks, Seek Advice

One way for you to step into your discomfort zone is to speak on other subjects when the opportunity arises, like I did on the cruise. Don't let the opportunity pass. Your hands may shake and your knees knock, but say—YES anyway.

Years ago, as a new speaking coach, I needed more visibility on bigger stages. One day, I was invited to present at a morning breakout session during a large seminar. I was excited since this was a great way to get started. I was shocked when they told me I had to pay $1,250 and give them half of everything I sold for the privilege.

"What?!" I thought. "Speakers get paid to speak, not the other way around."

I called my mentor.

He said, "It's a small price to pay to break into the industry."

So I paid. The result? Several influential industry leaders invited me to speak on their stages.

After you succeed, celebrate. Pat yourself on the back and say, "Good job." You stepped into your discomfort zone.

25

Keep Your Cool When Your Speech Goes Up in Flames

Expect challenges, go with the flow, and give a great speech anyway.
--Arvee Robinson

When you speak in public, problems will arise, spin out of control, and mess up your confidence. Use these cool public speaking techniques to keep your speech from going up in flames.

1. Your PowerPoint doesn't work

PowerPoint creates a higher level of complexity. One of the biggest problems you will encounter is equipment incompatibility. One speaker on my stage was adamant about using PowerPoint. However, when we plugged our projector into his Apple computer, we discovered they were incompatible. With the audience waiting and the speaker sweating, five computer buffs in the audience offered their help. It took 30 minutes to fix the problem. The commotion shattered the event's momentum. When the speaker stepped on stage the energy in the room had plummeted. He was unable to regain the audience's rapport and, as a result, made no sales.

I once experienced the same problem. Ten minutes before I stepped on stage at a multi-speaker event, I discovered a PowerPoint incompatibility problem. I didn't sweat because I knew my material and I never rely on PowerPoint. While the gurus sweated, I started my speech on time, connected with the audience, and built rapport with my story. Fifteen minutes later, when the gurus solved the problem, I jumped back into the PowerPoint slides so smoothly the audience never noticed.

On another occasion, I was invited to speak on a large stage with a big screen behind me. I planned to use PowerPoint because over 200 people were expected. This event met all the PowerPoint criteria: I had 90 minutes to speak, I was selling from the platform, I had the best speaking time right before lunch, and a large audience.

Fifteen people showed up. It would've looked ridiculous for me to present my PowerPoint on the huge screen for so few people. I dumped the slide show, stepped off stage to get closer to my audience, and delivered my speech. This created a memorable, intimate experience for my audience instead of a laughable one.

2. A big space with few people

I shared with you how I handled having a big stage and a tiny audience. In that situation I decided not to use my PowerPoint but instead walked off stage and down into the audience to speak.

Not long ago, I was invited to be a guest speaker at a major event at the Rio Hotel in Las Vegas featuring many top speakers. They expected over 600 attendees. I was excited to share the stage with speaking giants such as Tommy Hopkins, Marshall Sylver, Larry Benet, and Berny Dohrmann.

I arrived early to get a front row seat in the main ballroom before the crowd showed up. Chandeliers sparkled from ceiling, adding to the beauty of the room. Behind the VIP tables, hundreds of empty chairs in perfect rows waited in silence to be filled. I anticipated stepping onto the vast stage with its curtained black velvet background.

The nine o'clock start time came and went. By nine-fifteen a dozen or so people had trickled into the room. At nine-thirty, with forty-four people scattered around the room, the event started.

Because there were so few people in the room, I asked the audience to bring their chairs and sit in theater style close to the stage. I turned a big empty room into a small intimate gathering.

Don't be afraid to take charge. When a difficult situation arises, ask your audience to do whatever is necessary to create a great experience.

3. A heckler in the room

Hecklers are the problem children in your audience. You may not have one every time you speak but when you do they will let you know they are there.

A heckler is negative, demands attention, challenges your knowledge, and asks too many questions.

You must defuse any heckler fast or you will lose control of your audience, your speech, and yourself. Defuse them with a compliment or a polite command.

You will meet several types of hecklers.

Use a compliment to defuse a know-it-all. This kind of heckler wants to be acknowledged and will chatter and ask questions to get attention.

You can say, "It sounds like you have a lot of experience in this area. I'm going to talk about that later. When the time comes, would it be alright if I call on you?"

They will nod in agreement and be silent. The secret? You never call on them. When they come up to you afterwards, smile and say, "Oh, I apologize. I forgot."

Use a polite command to defuse an over-achiever. This type of heckler rushes to the stage every time you ask for a volunteer.

You can say, "Thank you. However, I'm looking for someone who hasn't participated yet." If it's a man, you can say, 'Thank you. Let's hear from a woman." That way he no longer qualifies.

4. People talk during your presentation

Stop talking. The talkers will look up because you are quiet. Smile and continue your presentation.

One time when I became silent, a group in the back of the room kept talking and didn't notice the silence. I said, "Excuse me in the back of the room. Hello!" I said it a couple times until I got their attention. "Excuse me, could you give us the same respect that we gave you?" They quieted down. The audience applauded. For the next two days, people talked about the polite, positive way I took control of the room.

5. Your time has been cut

This has happened to me many times and it will happen to you. When other speakers take too much time or the organizer adds an item to the program, the domino effect leaves less time for you to speak.

What can you do? First, be grateful for the time you have. Second, remove a few pieces of meat from your speech sandwich to fit the available time.

Don't rewrite your presentation. Reduce the meat and leave the bread (your rapport and your close).

Don't tell your audience your time was cut or rush through your speech. Present at a normal pace. Your audience will never know the difference. Be professional. Never blame the organizer if you want to speak there again.

6. Your shoe gets caught on the stage

This is not be a problem for men, but it can be for women speakers who wear skinny high heels. Most stages are made from blocks crisscrossed with narrow openings that are hungry to grab one of those heels. One stiletto-wearing speaker walked right into one of these openings, walked out of her shoes, and delivered her entire presentation barefoot. It didn't help her professionalism or her sales. It could have been worse. She could have fallen flat on her face.

Ladies, if your heel gets stuck on the stage, make a simple joke about it, take it out, keep your shoes on, ask the staff to tape the stage, and continue to speak. You can't give a great presentation if you are worried about your shoe getting caught by the stage.

When you arrive at the venue, check the stage and make sure the hotel staff tapes the seams before you start your presentation.

These are a few of the many challenges speakers encounter. No matter what happens, the key to success is to stay cool, calm, and collected. Never let your audience see you sweat.

26

Get Engaged!

If you don't ask for a speaking engagement, the answer is already no.
--Arvee Robinson

You've crafted your signature talk. Now it's time to get speaking engagements.

To achieve the greatest results from public speaking, first identify the people you want to do business with. Identify potential organizations, associations, and companies within a 25-mile radius of your home or office where your target market, your ideal clients and customers, gather. Donavan did this when he created his own caravan meeting and got in front of real estate professionals. Jill found her target market at Whole Foods Market. Like Donavan and Jill, find out where your prospects hang out and go there to speak.

Next, create a spreadsheet to capture important information such as: Name of organization, name of program chair or president, date and time of meeting, phone number, email address, website, and a comment field. This will assist you when contacting them.

Once you've identified where you want to speak, before you contact the organization create a "one-sheet" describing your talk and the value their audience will get from your presentation. A one-sheet is one piece of paper, front and back. Include these critical elements: title of your talk, your name, five bullet points showing the benefits the audience will receive, a testimonial, your bio, your picture, and your contact information. Don't create expensive marketing materials. Instead, create a simple Word document, and convert it to PDF format you can send by email to a prospective organizer. For an example, see Appendix 4.

Next, schedule the speaking engagement. Use my ATM approach.

A stands for ASK. Because many organizations only invite members to speak, call each one on your list and ask if they invite outside speakers. If yes, find out who schedules speakers and share with that person how your topic benefits the group. Be courteous, professional, and focus on the organization's needs, not yours. Organizations put their reputation on the line when they invite you to speak. They want to look good and know they made the right decision.

The T is for TELL. When you introduce yourself at a networking meeting, tell the group you are a speaker looking for places to speak.

The M is for MAIL. Mail your one-sheet to the organizations you identified earlier.

One of my clients used this strategy and got over 25 paid speaking engagements.

Grace owns a successful consulting company. Her heart's desire was to speak to women in churches who were experiencing challenges they couldn't resolve on their own. She identified 100 churches within a 25-mile radius of her home and mailed her one-sheet and a cover letter to each one. Grace didn't plan to charge for her talk. She was surprised when several churches called to ask how much she charged. These churches offered to pay her an honorarium of $250 to $500 per talk. Never underestimate the power of direct mail marketing.

Once your targeted organization says yes, email your one-sheet, your speaker introduction (see Appendix 2) and your picture. The organization will use this information when marketing their upcoming event. Make their job easy by sending your information as soon as you get off the phone.

27

The Biggest Lie

*Like any profession, you must pay your dues
before you can expect to get paid.*
--Arvee Robinson

Attend one speech class and get paid thousands of dollars to speak.

Lie, lie, lie.

You will be lucky to even speak for free anywhere. No program chair wants a speaker with no experience or reputation to make them look bad.

The stories you hear about speakers who get paid a lot of money for speaking mostly involve athletes, celebrities, high former government officials, or people with dramatic physical defects.

These people are extremely rare. You on the other hand, no matter what business you are in, are one among many thousands of people attempting to get on one of these few high-paying stages.

If you are an actor fresh out of acting school, you would not expect to get a lead role for a million dollars in a major movie. This would be ridiculous. Yet an inspiring speaker takes one class and expects to be paid thousands. This is super ridiculous.

Expect to speak for free on a lot of small stages for years and build your reputation, experience, and message.

Build relationships, trust and rapport, and give great value on at least 200 stages before you ever ask for a dime in return. Use these speeches to build your database, generate leads, and get referrals.

Focus on cultivating special relationships with influencers in every organization you speak to. If you do this, you will begin to attract higher-level speaking opportunities, and in time even get paid.

Along the way, some organizations will offer to pay you a small honorarium that can range from $25 to $500. Accept it with gratitude.

Brian Tracy, motivational speaker, personal development trainer and author, and one of the highest paid speakers in America, started this way. After 50 years on stage he now requires a speaking fee of $35,000 or higher, plus expenses.

Tony Hsieh, CEO of Zappos in Las Vegas became an overnight celebrity when his online shoe business took off. Because he made so much money in so little time people wanted to know how he did it. Even though he did not want to speak, he received numerous speaking invitations, so many that he raised his speaking fee to $75,000 per talk hoping to discourage people from asking. They still ask.

Becoming one of these highly-paid speakers is like expecting an average high school basketball star become an NBA pro. The odds are 100,000 to 1.

This doesn't mean you can't make money. I've made a fortune by using speaking as a marketing strategy to generate leads and attract clients. I've also made hundreds of thousands of dollars selling my products and services from the platform. This is a far more reliable source of income than an occasional paid speaking engagement.

Your personal journey will be unique to you.

There is no magic recipe for success, even in speaking. No one can make you a success. You must make your own way, taking advantage of every opportunity, and create as many of your own opportunities as you can.

Keep learning, practicing, and taking action every day toward your speaking goals. One day you will be paid the big bucks. No lie.

Part VI

Experience Your Power as a
Speaker and Leader

28

Messages of Leaders Who Have Left a Legacy

A powerful message will live forever.
--Arvee Robinson

Throughout history, great communicators, speaking with confidence and influence, have changed laws, accomplished the impossible, and saved lives.

Let's look at messages from three world-change leaders.

Dr. Christine Horner is a plastic surgeon and breast cancer specialist from San Diego, California. Many of her early patients had had a mastectomy and needed reconstructive surgery. She was outraged when she discovered that insurance companies refused to pay for this surgery.

Dr. Horner was so passionate about ending this refusal that she left her practice and started the Breast Reconstruction Advocacy Project, which developed into a five-year national campaign to advocate passage of laws requiring such payments. She appeared on radio, television, including Oprah, on stages, and in dozens of national magazines to bring her message to a wide audience.

Because of her dedication, on October 21, 1998 President Bill Clinton signed a federal law requiring insurance companies to pay for reconstructive surgery after a mastectomy. Thirty-five states passed similar laws.

Dr. Horner is a change-leader whose brave words, conviction, and determination changed laws and restored confidence and beauty to women all over the country.

Martin Luther King Jr. transformed his role as a local Baptist minister, speaker, and community leader, into serving as a national activist, humanitarian, and one of the most powerful leaders of the African-American Civil Rights Movement. He gave his life to fulfill his passion.

He delivered his most famous speech, *I have a Dream*, to hundreds of small local audiences before he was ready to deliver it one last time to hundreds of thousands of civil rights supporters in front of the Lincoln Memorial in Washington D.C.

Speaking ran in his family. His father was a minister, his grandfather was a minister and he first learned speaking skills by sitting in church listening to two great preachers, his father and his grandfather. As soon as they would let him, he was teaching Sunday school and never looked back.

In 1954, Dr. King became pastor of the Dexter Avenue Baptist Church in Montgomery, Alabama, and used that pulpit to advocate for civil rights. He soon joined the executive committee of the National Association for the Advancement of Colored People (NAACP).

On December 1, 1955, after working all day as a seamstress in a sweat shop, Rosa Parks boarded a bus to go home. Minutes after Rosa sat down in the row behind the white section, three white men entered. Segregation was heavily enforced and bus drivers were allowed to carry guns. Bus driver James Blake asked her to give up her seat. Rosa Parks refused.

She was arrested and fined for breaking segregation laws.

This incident sparked the Montgomery Bus Boycott and ignited the modern Civil Rights Movement.

Dr. King began to speak at local town hall meetings, schools, and churches. He then organized nonviolent protests and marches that attracted national attention after televised news captured brutal police violence that erupted in Selma, Alabama.

After all these years of preparation he was ready on August 28, 1963 to deliver his most famous speech, *I Have a Dream*. It was there that he established his reputation as one of the greatest speakers in American History.

Dr. King spent his entire life getting ready for this one moment. As a result, the landmark Civil Rights Act was passed in 1964 and the Voting Rights Act in 1965.

Martin Luther King Jr. gave us hope, led a movement, changed laws, and saved lives with his words. That's the mark of a true leader.

Candy Lightner was not a speaker, leader, or public figure. She was a divorced mother of three who lived in a small town and sold real estate to support her children.

On May 3, 1980, at 4:00 pm after shopping with friends, Candy returned home to find her dad, ex-husband Steve, and neighbors sitting on the front porch. She got out of her car and Steve walked up and held her tight.

"What's wrong," she asked.

Steve said, "We've lost Cari."

"We'll find her," Candy said. "She's at a neighbor's house."

Steve looked her in the eye. "She's dead. She was hit by a car and she is dead."

Candy collapsed in his arms.

She later learned that her 13-year-old daughter was walking to a Church carnival with a friend when a drunk driver hit her from behind, so hard she was thrown 125 feet and died instantly. The 47-year-old driver fled. His wife later turned him in to police after she saw him wipe blood off his front bumper.

The man who killed her little girl was a repeat offender who had been released on bail on a hit and run charge only two days before Cari's death.

Four days after her daughter's tragedy, the day after her funeral, Candy was shocked to discover this was his fifth offense in four years. He spent less than two days in jail for killing Cari. She exploded. "This will never happen to any other child again!"

The next day, still overwhelmed with anger, she let a couple of her girlfriends take her out to lunch. "It's horrible, two days in jail is all he got, I can't believe it!" She said with tears in her eyes. One of her friends put her arm around her. She exploded again, stared straight at her friends, "I'm so mad. We've got to do something about this, we've got to do it now." Her friends stared back at her for a few seconds. And one of them said, "So let's do it now." Candy looked up and said, "Yes." She said. "I'm so mad---mad! That's it, we will call it MADD!"

One of her friends said, "We are all mothers."

"And we are all against drunk drivers." Candy said. "That's it! Mothers Against Drunk Drivers."

The three women stood, held hands across the table and smiled at each other for the first time in days. "We can do this, and we'll make 'em pay."

She started MADD, Mothers Against Drunk Drivers, later changed to Mothers Against Drunk Driving, a non-profit organization dedicated to raising public awareness of the seriousness of drunk driving and to create tougher laws.

She started by speaking to anyone who would listen, local neighborhood groups, service clubs, and business groups. She fought for change on radio and television shows including *Nightline* and *Good Morning America*. Mothers from all over America joined her cause. She even spoke to the United States Congress. Within two years MADD grew to over 100 chapters nationwide.

Because of her tenacity, over time every state lowered blood alcohol concentration levels from .10 to .08 and raised the drinking age from 18 to 21. As a result, alcohol-related deaths have declined an estimated 900 per year. Over the past 30 years, Candy's crusade has saved over 27,000 lives. Her new organization, We Save Lives, coordinates groups that oppose drugged and distracted driving.

29

Speak Up and Lead

Your words create the world around you.
--Arvee Robinson

Not everyone reaches the top. However, public speaking has the potential to take you as high as you want to go. When used consistently, it will transform you from unknown to well-known in your industry.

This happened to Lee. Lee was a genealogy enthusiast. One summer at the age of 24, he went to Germany and found his German ancestors, which is difficult to do. At the next meeting of his local genealogy society he mentioned his success to one of the members. A few days later the program chair called and asked him to give a presentation to the entire society (a one-hour talk in front of 150 people). The talk, his first ever, was a success and Lee left thinking nothing further of it. Two days later the phone rang. It was the program chair of another society. "I heard you speak the other day. I loved your program. Would you give that talk to our society?" He said yes.

In less than a week, he went from unknown to perceived expert in this field. The day before his speech, he knew as much about the subject as he did the day after. The difference? He went from no one knowing who he was to being in demand. Eventually, he spoke to every society in Southern California and at regional conferences and seminars. He soon became well-known and one of the top leaders in the industry.

When you are trained, practice, and develop your speech according to my system, this can happen to you too.

Marry your knowledge with your passion and share it with the right audience, which is what Lee did, and your message will explode throughout your industry and beyond. You become an attractor who draws people to you and your message. Many who hear you will invite you to speak or spread the word.

This happened to me.

It was 7:20 a.m. and I was praying someone would show up for my early morning breakout session. My prayers were answered and by 7:30 a.m. it was standing room only. One of the participants, who I had noticed standing in the back of the room, hung out after my presentation until most of the crowd left. Then he approached me. "How would you like to speak on my stage?" he asked. What else could I say? "Yes!"

This has happened again and again throughout my career. Now, the opportunities, stages, and audiences get bigger and bigger. I never call to find speaking engagements, they call me.

When you become a known leader in your industry, you also take on great responsibility. People perceive you as an industry expert. You must continue to master your skills, keep your passion burning, and your content current.

Now is the time to lead. You have a life-changing message that only you can share with people who can only hear it from

YOU. They are waiting for your words. If you don't deliver your message, it will remain undelivered for all eternity.

30

Your Next Step to Success

Training is fundamental to your speaking success.
--Arvee Robinson

You can't see how other people see you when you speak. It may sound great to you, but it may not sound so great to your audience. The only way you can find out is to hire a third party coach or trainer to watch you speak and show you ways to improve the effectiveness of your speech.

The only way to get honest feedback is to hire the best coach in the business, a professional who is already a successful speaker and one who has trained thousands of people in the latest speaking trends and techniques.

You can either run with my speaker system and try to do it yourself or you can get professional training by me, in person, where I will walk you step-by-step through everything you need to know to master public speaking and be a success on the stage.

To take the next step, join my 4-day Speaker Training Intensive, which I present twice a year to a small group of carefully selected participants. It takes you from knowledge to having your money-making signature talk ready to go.

To apply for one of the exclusive seats, contact me at arvee@arveerobinson.com.

For more advanced training, you can apply to join my Million Dollar Messenger and Advanced Business-building Program, where you get private time with me, my signature four-day Speaker Training Intensive, accountability calls every month, and full access to me as needed.

This program is by invitation only. I work with a select number of people and spaces fill up fast. To apply, email me at milliondollarspeaker@arveerobinson.com

Thank you for taking the time to read this book. It's given you a far better understanding of what it takes to become a powerful presenter. As I've said many times in this book, the key to public speaking success is training, practicing, and stage time. In this book I have given you the foundation, systems, and techniques you need. Now it's time for you to get the training you need to become a success in your business.

Part VII

Appendices

SCRIPT FOR BOOKING SPEAKING ENGAGEMENTS

A: Script for speaking to chambers, associations, and organizations:

Hi, I am _____. My company is _____
        (Your name)   (Company name)
what we do is
_____
        (Your core message/elevator speech)

The reason why I am calling is to see if you invite guest speakers to come and speak to your group. Do you? (Silence). (If yes) Great!
My most popular topics include (List 3 different speech titles):
1) _____
2) _____
3) _____
Which topic do you think would most interest your group?

B: Script for speaking to companies/corporations

Hi, I am _____. My company is _____
        (Your name)   (Company name)
what we do is

_____
                (Your core message/elevator speech)

The reason why I am calling is because I am going to be in
your area next week and I want to offer you a 30-minute
complimentary presentation. My most popular topics include (List
3 different speech titles):
1) _____
2) _____
3) _____
How do you feel about me coming out and speaking to your
team?
(Silence)

C: Script for leaving a voice mail message:

Hi _____ This is _____
      (Name of person you are calling)   (Your name)
from _____
        (Your company name)
I have a quick question for you. Please call me back today at
_____, _____, Bye.
          (give your phone number, twice).

APPENDIX 2

WORKSHOP APPOINTMENT SETTING SCRIPT

Hi _____. This is _____ from
   (Repeat name if given)   (Your name)
_____.
  (Your company name)
Maybe you can help me. (People love to help).
Who would I speak with in regards to being a guest speaker at
your office? (Let them respond.)
May I speak with _____ (say name of person in charge of
the meeting).
(Person answers.)
Hi, is _____ (say name of person in charge of the meeting)
in? (Let them respond.)
Hi, this is _____ _____.
          (Your full name)

This is _____(your name) I'm giving you a
quick call today to offer you and your team a 30-60 minute
customized training at your office on the topic of your choice.
The workshop is free.
The benefits to you are:
- Your team will receive a motivational, professional
  training. I normally charge $5,000 for a keynote speech.
  For a limited time, I'm offering companies a free
  customized training on the topic of your choice for no
  charge. I am doing this to build clientele in your area.
- Everyone in the meeting will get at least one great idea
  they can use immediately.

I am only able to do a limited number of these workshops. What
day and time would work best for you and your team?

(Let them respond).

How many people attend your meetings? (Let them respond).
If they say they have 5 or more people, say:

How do you feel about scheduling a workshop? (Let them
respond).

If they agree to the workshop, say:

Great, what is the address where the meeting will be held? What time does the meeting start?

I will send you an email confirmation. What is the best email address?

Do you have other offices in the area?

If I were to be a guest speaker at all of your locations, who would the person be to give me the green light?

SPEAKING ENGAGEMENT DATA SHEET

This tracks all the information you need to make this engagement a success

Your Speaking Date: _____

Organization:_____ Date of contact:_____

Contact name: _____ Phone: _____

Email address: _____ Cell Phone: _____

Meeting time: _____ to _____

Speaking time: _____ Length of talk: _____

(Circle one) Meeting: Breakfast, Lunch, or Dinner ? -

Speak before or after?

Address of speaking engagement:

_____

_____

Number of Attendees: _____ Men – Women - both

Profession of Attendees: _____Approx. age_____

Title of Talk:_____

Sent speaker introduction?: Yes, or No

Number of Handouts needed: _____

Free raffle gift(s):_____

Is this a Free or Paid Talk? If paic, how much $_____

APPENDIX 4

Arvee Robinson
The Master Speaker Trainer, International Speaker and Author

How to Use Public Speaking as a Marketing Strategy and Grow Your Business FAST!

Are you missing out on a TON of business because you are not speaking in front of groups?

Many business owners and service professionals struggle with speaking in front of groups. They struggle because they don't know what to say or how to say it. They are afraid of looking foolish. Consequently, they give up before they even try.
Don't let this happen. Instead, learn how to grow your business by giving persuasive presentations that attract clients to you!

In this presentation, you will learn how to:
- Grow your business every time you speak.
- Build your database and market to it forever.
- Get more speaking engagements than you can handle.
- Generate unlimited qualified leads.
- Look like a seasoned pro even if you don't feel like one.

"Arvee Robinson is one of the top speaker trainers in the world. I highly recommend her programs to anyone who wants to become a great front of the room speaker."- Eric Lofholm, Sales Trainer

Arvee Robinson is the Master Speaker Trainer, international speaker, and author. She teaches business owners, service professionals, and entrepreneurs how to use public speaking as a marketing strategy so they can attract more clients, generate unlimited leads, grow their businesses, and get their message out to the world. Arvee has delivered over 3,500 speeches, 500 seminars and countless teleseminars. As a high-energy motivational speaker, Arvee has shared the stage with speaking giants such as Mark Victor Hansen, Loral Langemeier, and many more. Arvee offers private coaching, workshops, weekly teleclasses, and year-long mastermind programs. Her speaker training programs transform ordinary business owners into superstars in their industry and they make money for the rest of their lives.

Speaker One-sheet Template:

(Your Name and Title)

Title of Your Speech

State the potential problem as a question. (Is this happening to them?)

State the pain and suffering caused by the problem and show understanding.

Solve The problem.

In this presentation, you will learn how to: (Outline or Bullet points):

Picture	Bio

Add your contact information in the footer of the page

APPENDIX 5

SPEAKER INTRODUCTION TEMPLATE

I would like to introduce our guest speaker, ***Arvee Robinson***. Arvee is The Master Speaker Trainer, international speaker and author. She teaches business owners and entrepreneurs how to generate unlimited leads, attract more clients, and grow their business fast by delivering persuasive presentations.

Arvee is here today to share with us some great ideas on how you can **use public speaking as a marketing strategy to attract high-paying clients!**

Please join me in giving a warm welcome to ***Arvee Robinson!***

I would like to introduce our guest speaker _____.
                                                           (Full name)

_____ is a _____
   (First name)   (Title and/or credentials)

(She/he) _____
                        (Core message/elevator speech)

_____ is here today to share with us_____
 (First name)   (Speech title/benefits)
_____.

Please join me in giving a warm welcome to _____!
                                                           (Full name)

Note: Bring your introduction with you to your speaking engagement even if you previously emailed it to the organizer. When you arrive at your speaking location, find the person who is going to introduce you and have them read your introduction out loud in front to you. This way you know they have read it at least once, and if they have any questions you are there to answer them. Also, if necessary you can help them with the pronunciation of your name. This will set you up for speaking success.

Speaker Introduction Example With Large Type

I would like to introduce our guest speaker, **Arvee Robinson**.

Arvee is The Master Speaker Trainer, international speaker and author. She teaches Business Owners, and Entrepreneurs how to attract more clients, generate unlimited leads, and grow their businesses fast by delivering persuasive presentations. As a high-energy motivational speaker, Arvee has shared the stage with speaking giants such as Mark Victor Hansen, Tommy Hopkins, Loral Langemeier, and many, many more.

Arvee is here today to share with us some great ideas on **How to Use Public Speaking as a Marketing Strategy to Attract High-paying Clients**.

Please join me in giving a warm welcome to Arvee Robinson!

SPEAKER HANDOUT EXAMPLES

How Speaking Can Triple Your Business and Double Your Time Off!

Benefits of speaking:
1. Positions you as an _____
2. People get to _____, we buy from people we _____
3. People get to experience _____
4. It is an inexpensive _____
5. Easy way to build your _____ and market to them later

How do you get started?
1. Set a goal for _____ per month you want to give
2. Decide _____
3. Develop your _____

Where do you speak?
1. Local _____
2. _____ groups
3. Networking _____

Develop your talk:
1. Create a _____
2. Develop _____
3. Perfect the _____, give it _____

Arvee Robinson is The Master Speaker Trainer, international speaker, author, and founder of the Christian Speakers in Business Movement. She teaches business owners and entrepreneurs how to use public speaking as a marketing strategy so they can attract more clients, generate unlimited leads, and get their message out to the world and make a difference. A high-energy motivational speaker, Arvee has given over 3,500 speeches and has shared the stage with speaking giants, such as Mark Victor Hansen, Bernie Dorman, Tommy Hopkins, Loral Langemeier, Shellie Hunt, and the late Jay Conrad Levinson, and many more. Arvee offers private speech coaching, speaker training workshops, and public speaking mastermind programs.

How to Become a Persuasive Speaker

P _____
E _____
R _____
S _____
U _____
A _____
S _____
I _____
V _____
E _____
L _____
Y _____

Notes:

Arvee Robinson, is The Master Speaker Trainer, International Speaker, and Author. She teaches business owners, service professionals, and entrepreneurs how to use public speaking as a marketing strategy so they can attract more clients, generate unlimited leads, and grow their businesses, fast. She teaches a proven speaker system for delivering persuasive presentations, and easy formulas for creating killer elevator speeches and magnetic self-introductions. Arvee has given over 3,500 speeches all over the world and has trained over 5,000 individuals. She offers private coaching, workshops, weekly teleclasses and one-year mentoring and mastermind programs. Her programs will help you to make more sales for the rest of your life.

How to Use Public Speaking as a Marketing Strategy to Attract High-paying Clients!

L _____

E _____

A _____

D _____

S _____

3 mistakes speakers make that cost them money:

No _____

No _____

No _____

For information on Arvee's **4-day Speaker Training Intensive**
http://arveerobinson.com/training/speaker-training-intensive/

Arvee Robinson, is The Master Speaker Trainer, International Speaker, and Author. She teaches business owners, and entrepreneurs how to use public speaking as a marketing strategy so they can attract more clients, generate unlimited leads and grow their businesses, fast. She teaches a proven speaker system for delivering persuasive presentations, and easy formulas for creating killer elevator speeches and magnetic self-introductions. Arvee has helped hundreds of individuals to win clients and close more sales every time they speak. She offers private coaching, workshops, weekly teleclasses and one-year mentoring and mastermind programs. Her programs will make you money for the rest of your life.

COLLECTING BUSINESS CARD SCRIPT

How many of you like free stuff, by a show of hands?

Great!

I would like to give away this *(book, CD's, DVD's, Starbucks card)*, it contains _____ and sells for $_____ *($ value)*.

Everyone please take out a business card *(hold up a business card to show your audience).*

What I would like to do is add you to my database where you will receive a *(weekly/monthly)* _____ *(newsletter, video tip, quick tip)* on _____.

If you would like to be in the raffle but not on my list, simply fold the card in half. When I get to my office I will make sure you don't go in my database, sound good?

May I have a volunteer from the audience to help me collect the cards? *(Wait for someone to volunteer or pick someone).*

Great! What is your name? *(Ask the name of volunteer, shake hands and give them a collection bag, basket, or bowl).*

(To the Audience): (If sitting at round tables) Please pass your card to the person at your table with the longest hair or *(if it is a classroom setting)*: pass the cards to the center isle and

(Volunteer name) will pick them up.

(Volunteer) will you please pick a winner! *(Never select card yourself).*

(Volunteer picks and reads the name aloud).
Great! Let's give him/her and hand *(applause)*

(Give the volunteer the gift and you take the bag of cards and applause)

APPENDIX 8

CLOSING SCRIPT FOR FREE COACHING

What I would like to do is spend a few minutes and share with you how it works.

I gave all of you a half sheet of paper. It looks like this (hold up the half sheet). Take a moment and find your half sheet. Olympic athletes all have one thing in common. Do you know what it is?

That's right, a coach.

How many of you would agree by a show of hands that you would be more likely to follow through on your goals and commitments if you were working with a coach? *(Lead them by raising your hand).*

That is exactly why I offer my coaching program. To help people like you achieve your best. The free coaching session will last for 30 minutes.

At the end of the call I will share with you how my ongoing coaching program works.

There is no cost or any obligation to purchase coaching. Take a moment right now and where it asks for your name, jot down your name.

See where it asks for your phone number, jot down the best number to reach you. And where it asks for your email, jot down your email address.

Has everyone completed their form that would like a free coaching session?

Great. Take a moment and pass your coaching forms to the center aisle.

Those of you who filled out a form will receive a call from my office in the next day or two to set up your coaching call.

APPENDIX 9

FREE COACHING FORM SAMPLE:
"NO-OBLIGATION COACHING REGISTRATION FORM"

☐Yes, I am interested in a FREE 30-minute coaching session. . . . I want to

attract more clients today by learning the secrets of persuasive speaking. Also, I want to learn how to command my audience's attention, gain confidence, deliver overwhelming value, and end with an irresistible call to action.

CONTACT INFORMATION

First Name   Last Name

Billing Address

City   State   City   Zip Code

Phone   Phone (Alternate)

E-mail Address (PLEASE PRINT)   Website Address

Best time to reach you:

Arvee Robinson, The Master Speaker Trainer, (909) 949-8527
www.arveerobinson.com

APPENDIX 10

THE MILLION DOLLAR SPEAKER SYSTEM ™

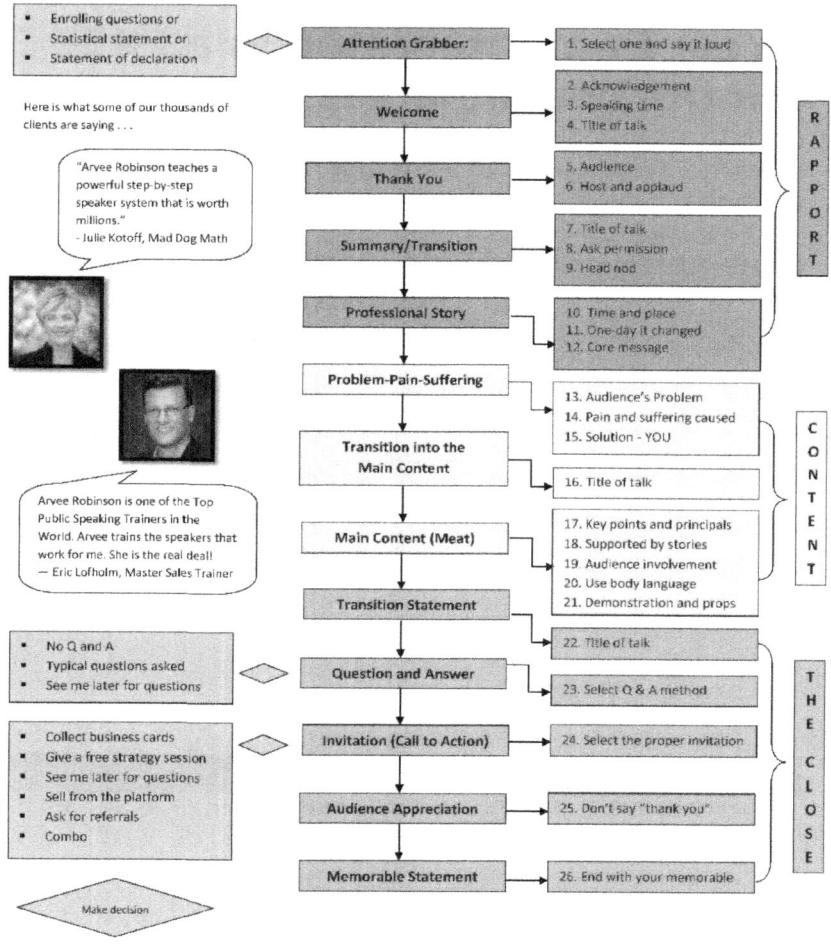

Made in the USA
Las Vegas, NV
25 March 2022